MANDALA MADNESS

ADULT COLORING BOOK

KYMIE EDWINS

WELCOME TO MANDALA MADNESS

This coloring book contains 50 black and white mandalas for your coloring
pleasure. You may use any coloring materials you wish.

ABOUT THE AUTHOR

Kymie Edwins is a Creative Director based in New York City. Aside from watching Broadway Musicals, she spends her time saving the world one pixel at a time, or at least that's what she thinks.

http://www.KyimeEdwins.com

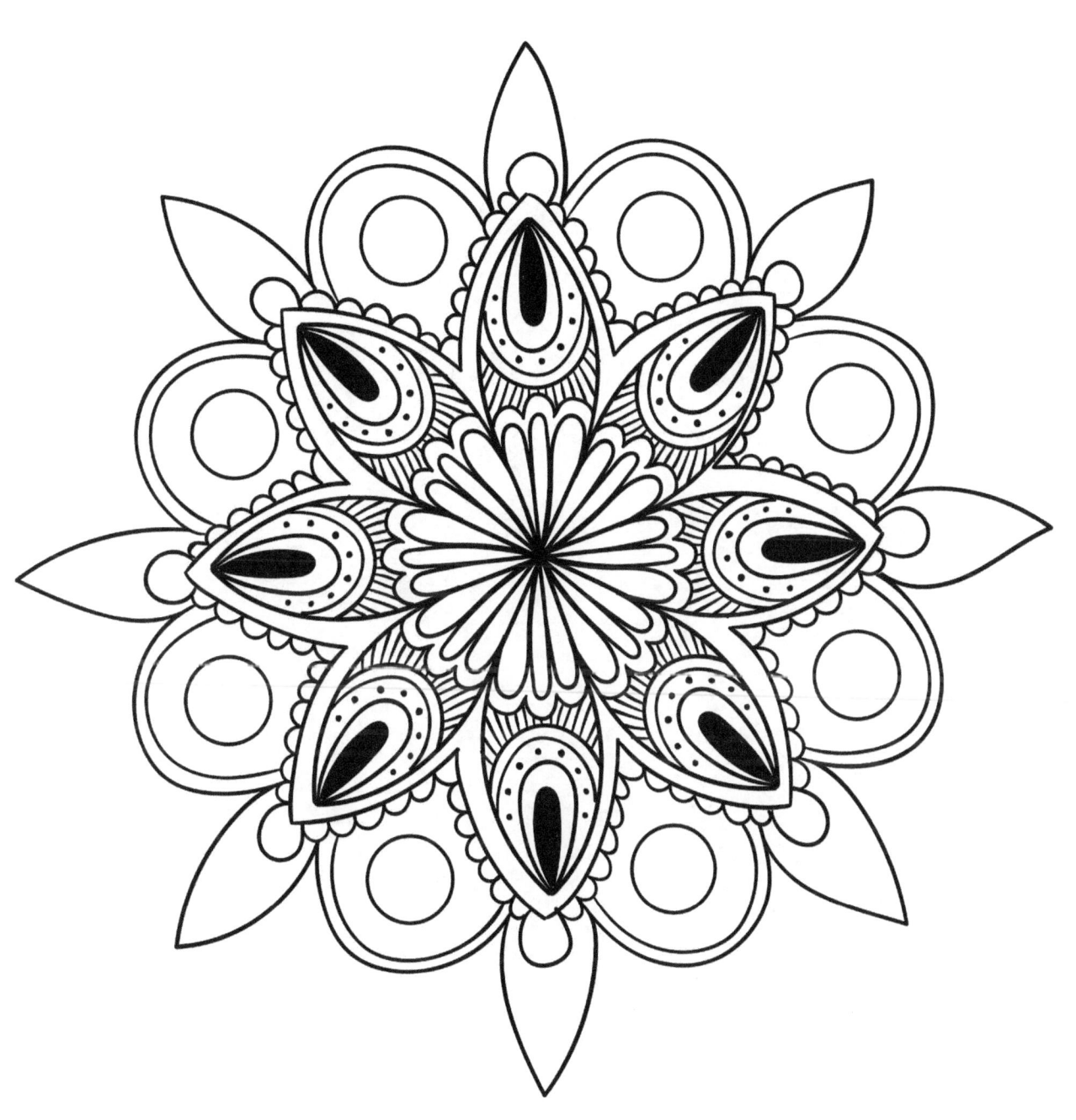

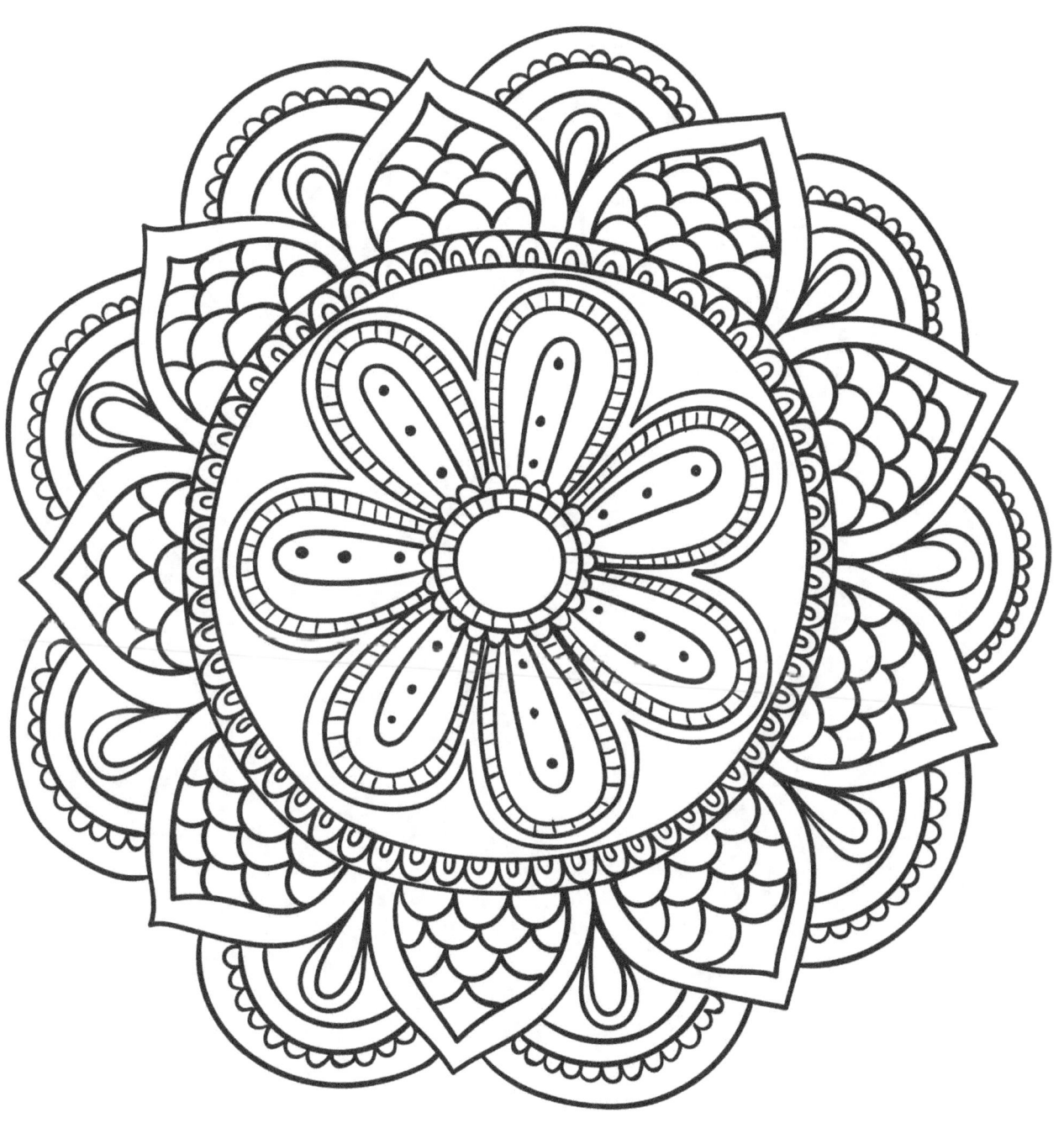

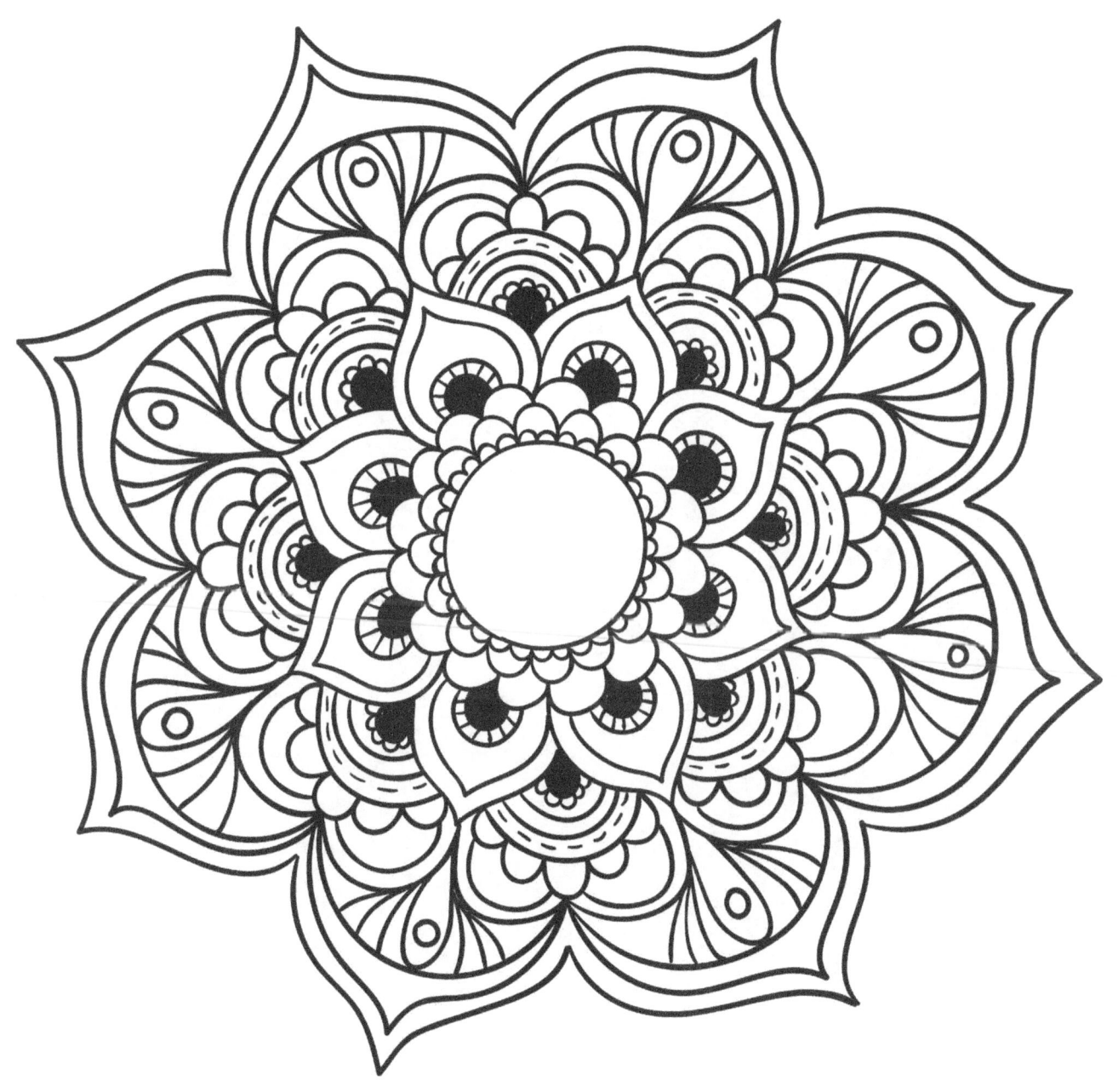

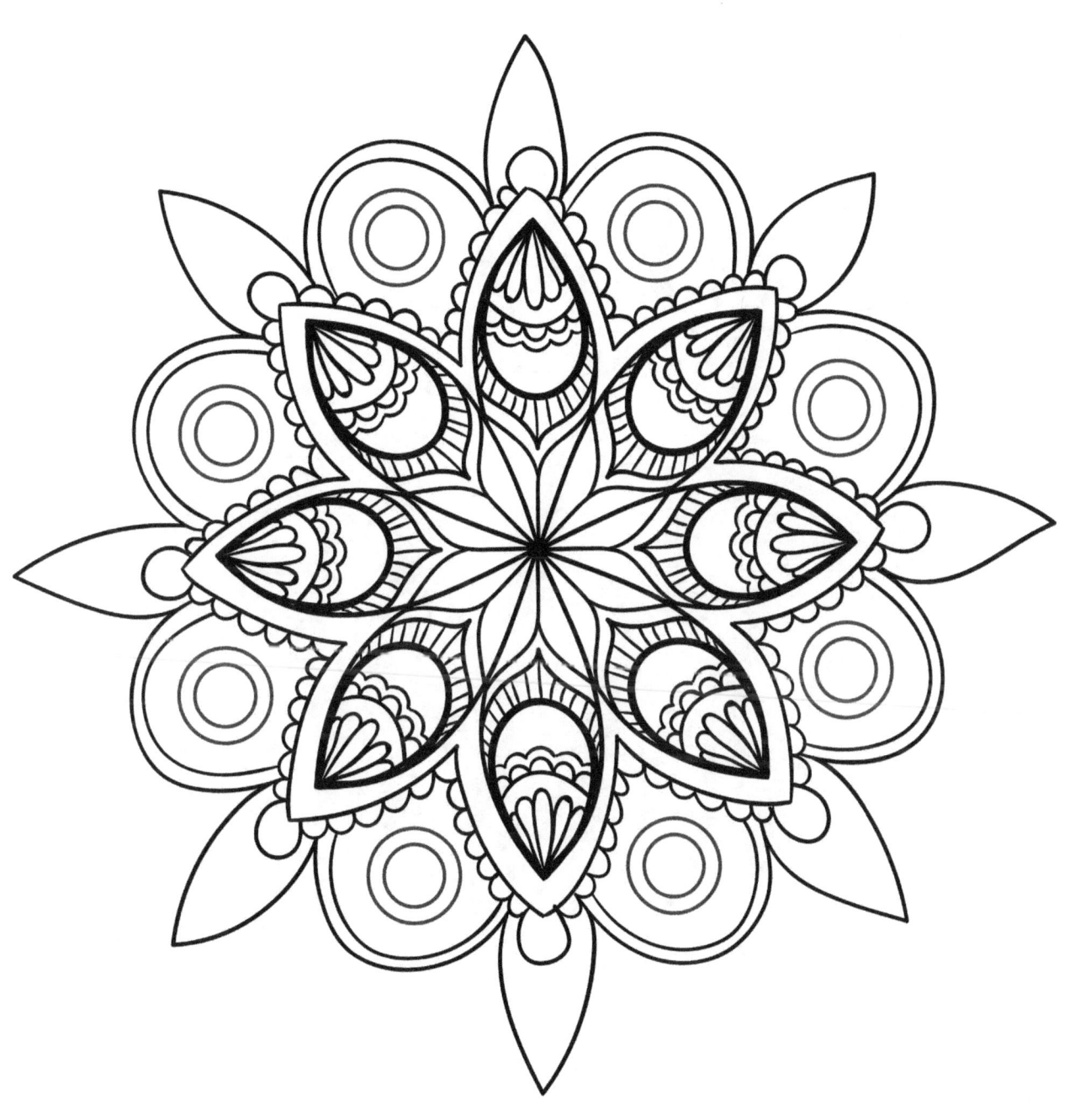

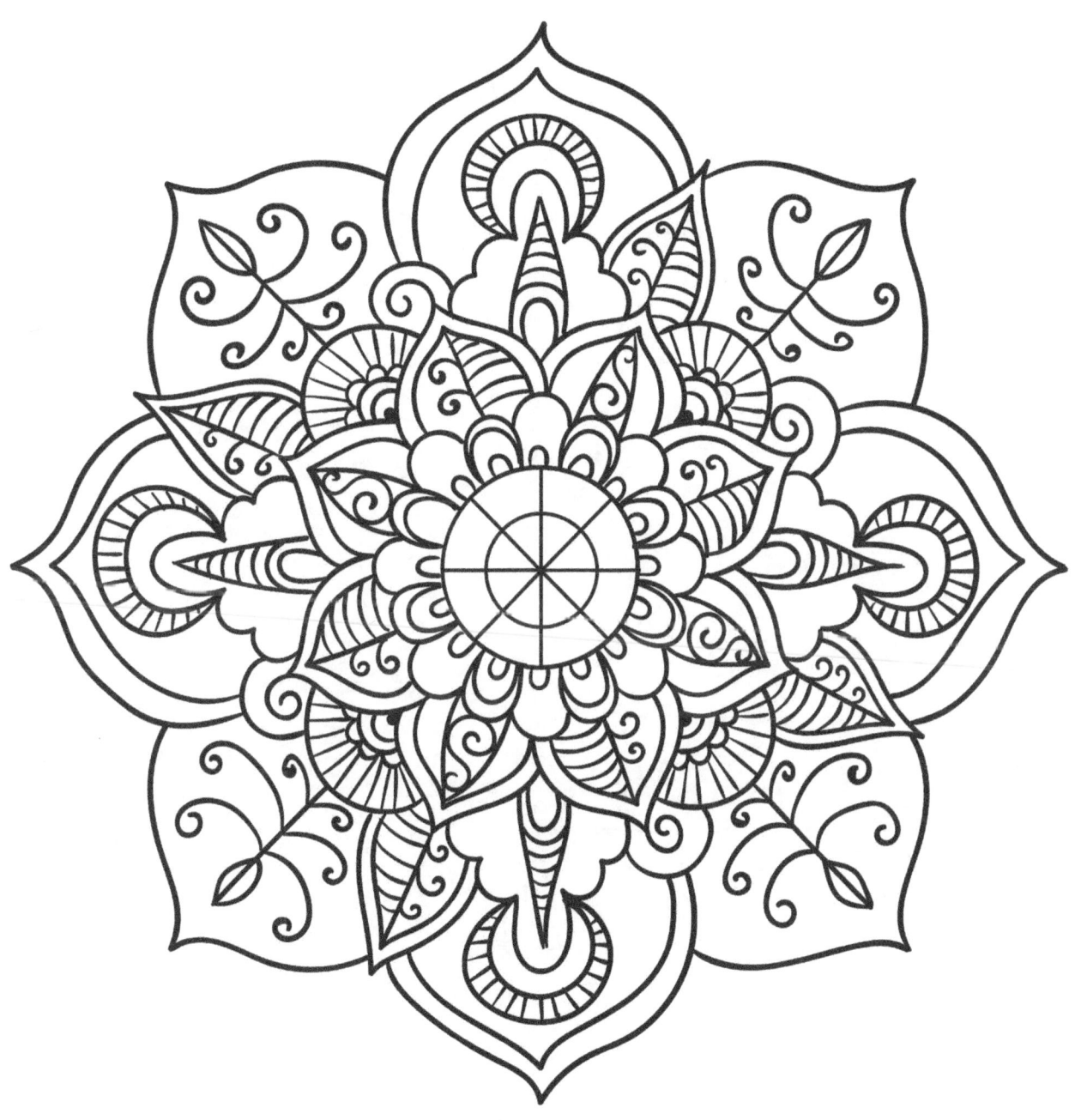

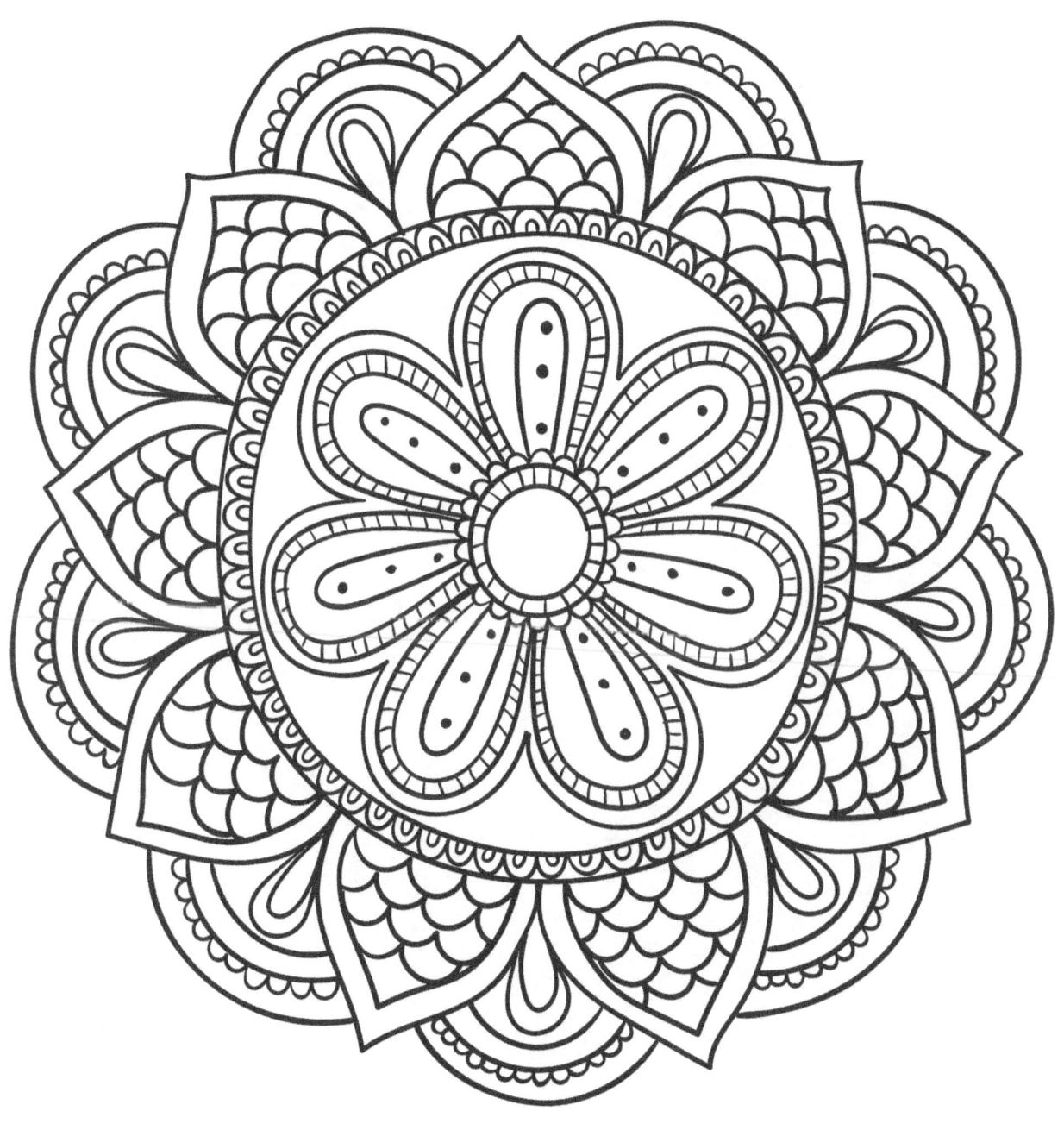

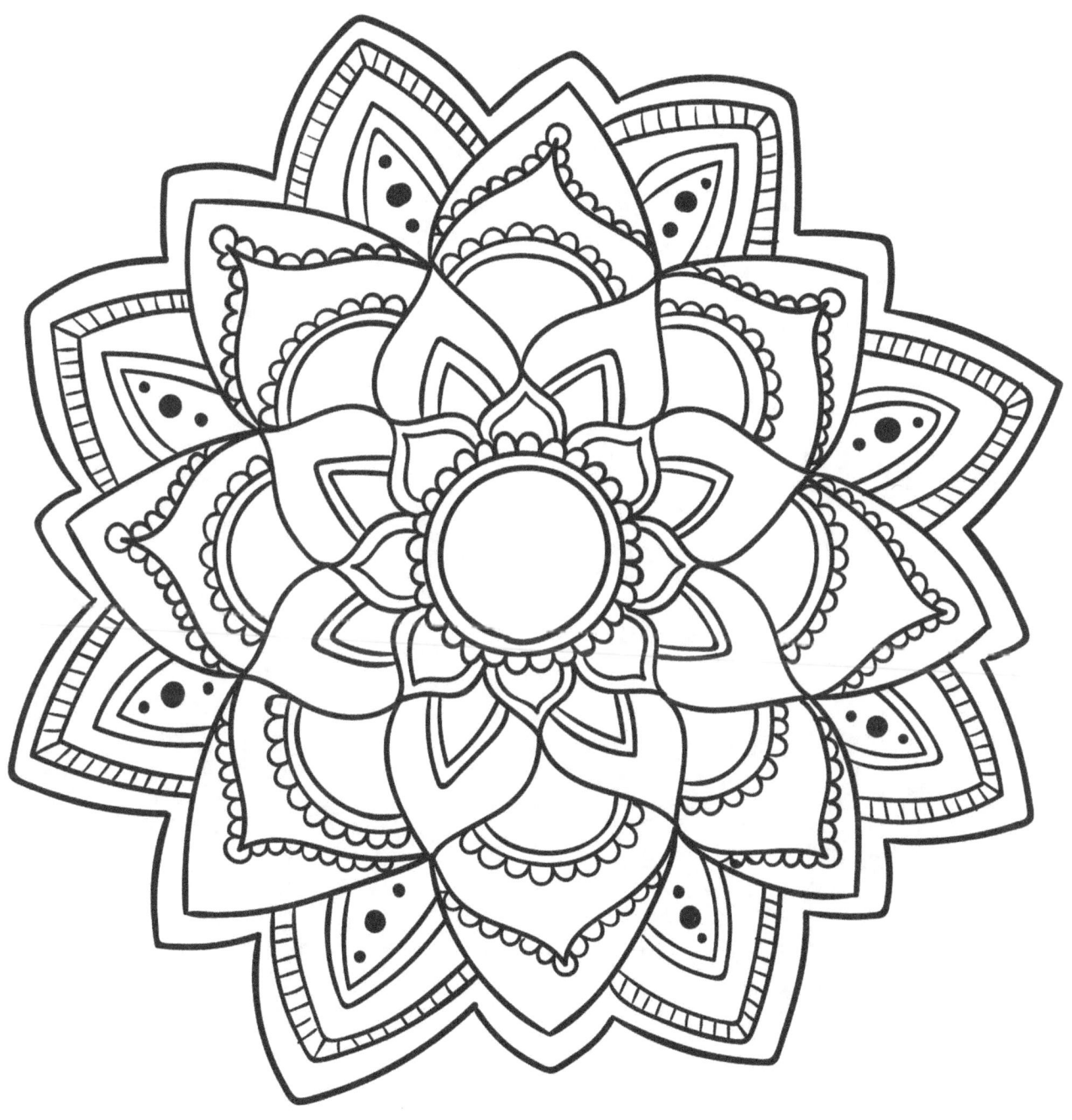

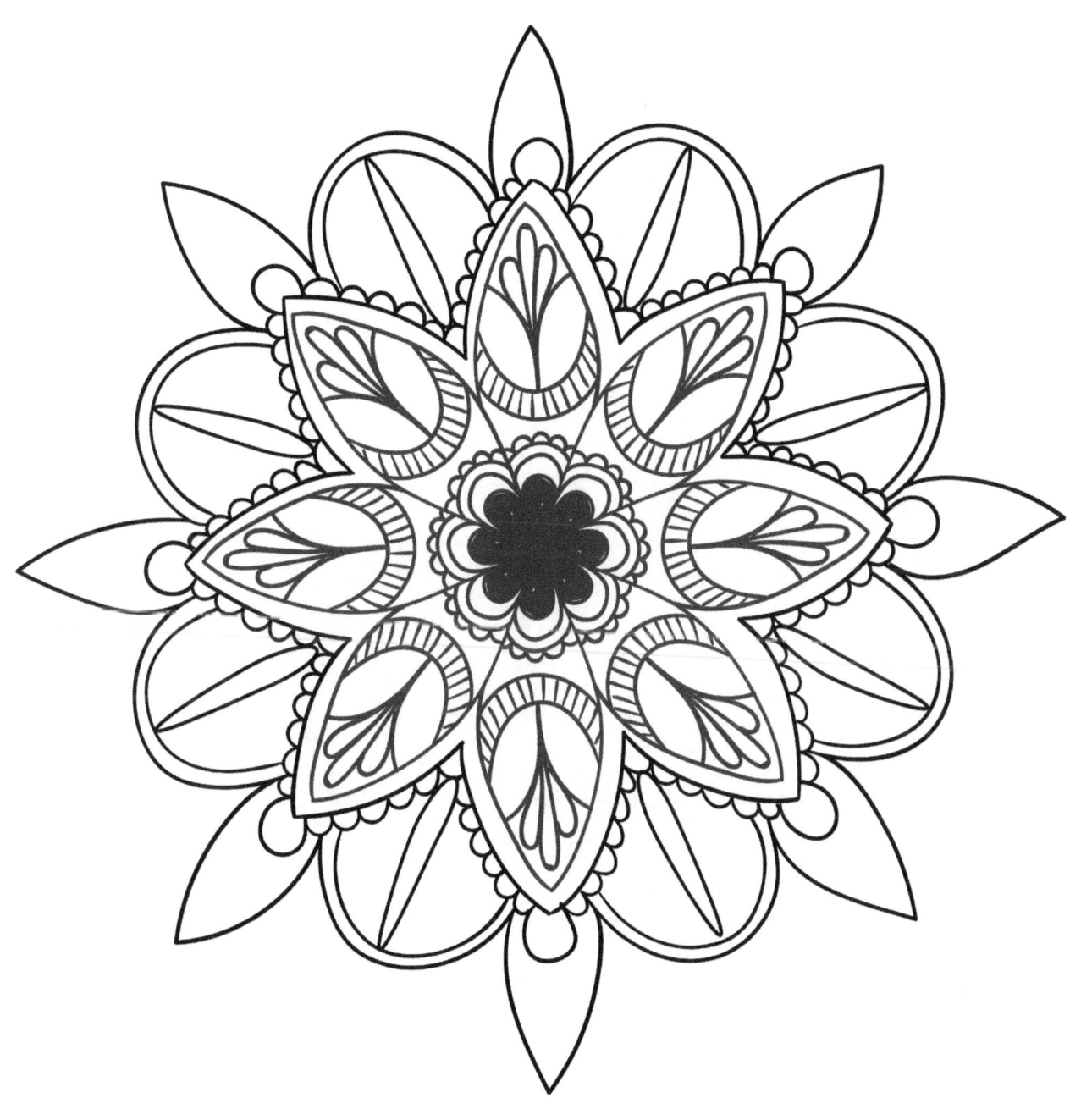

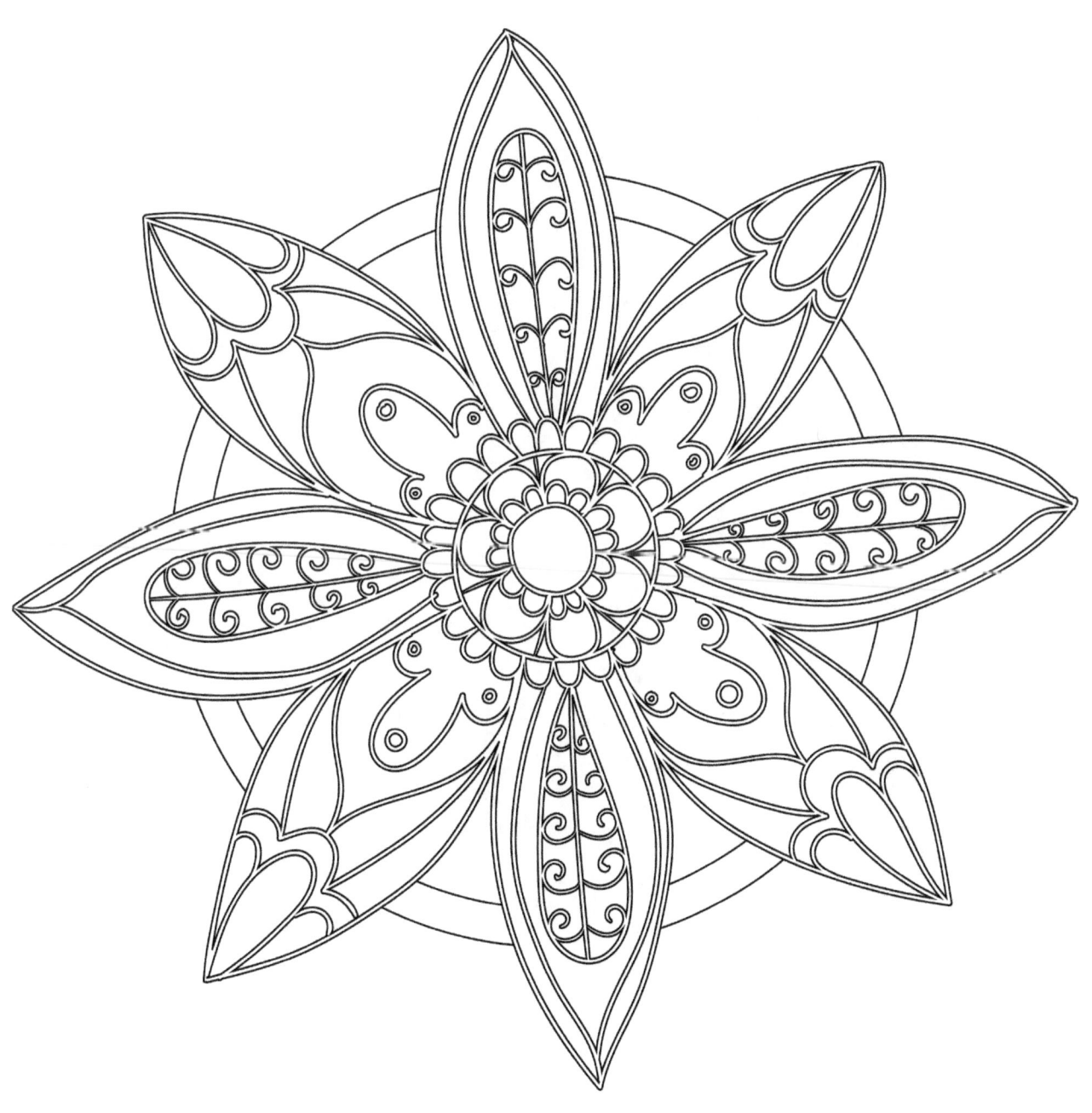

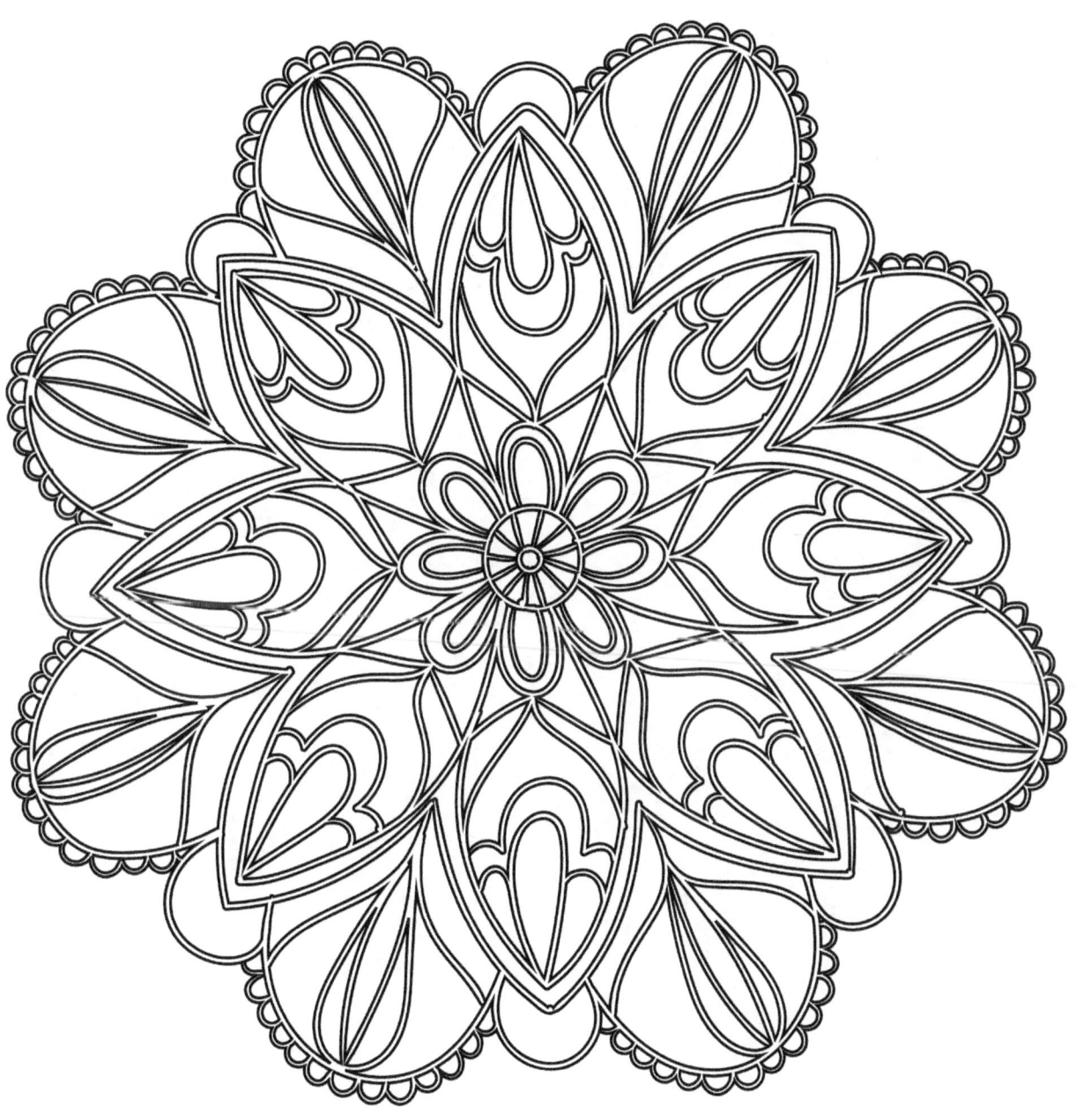

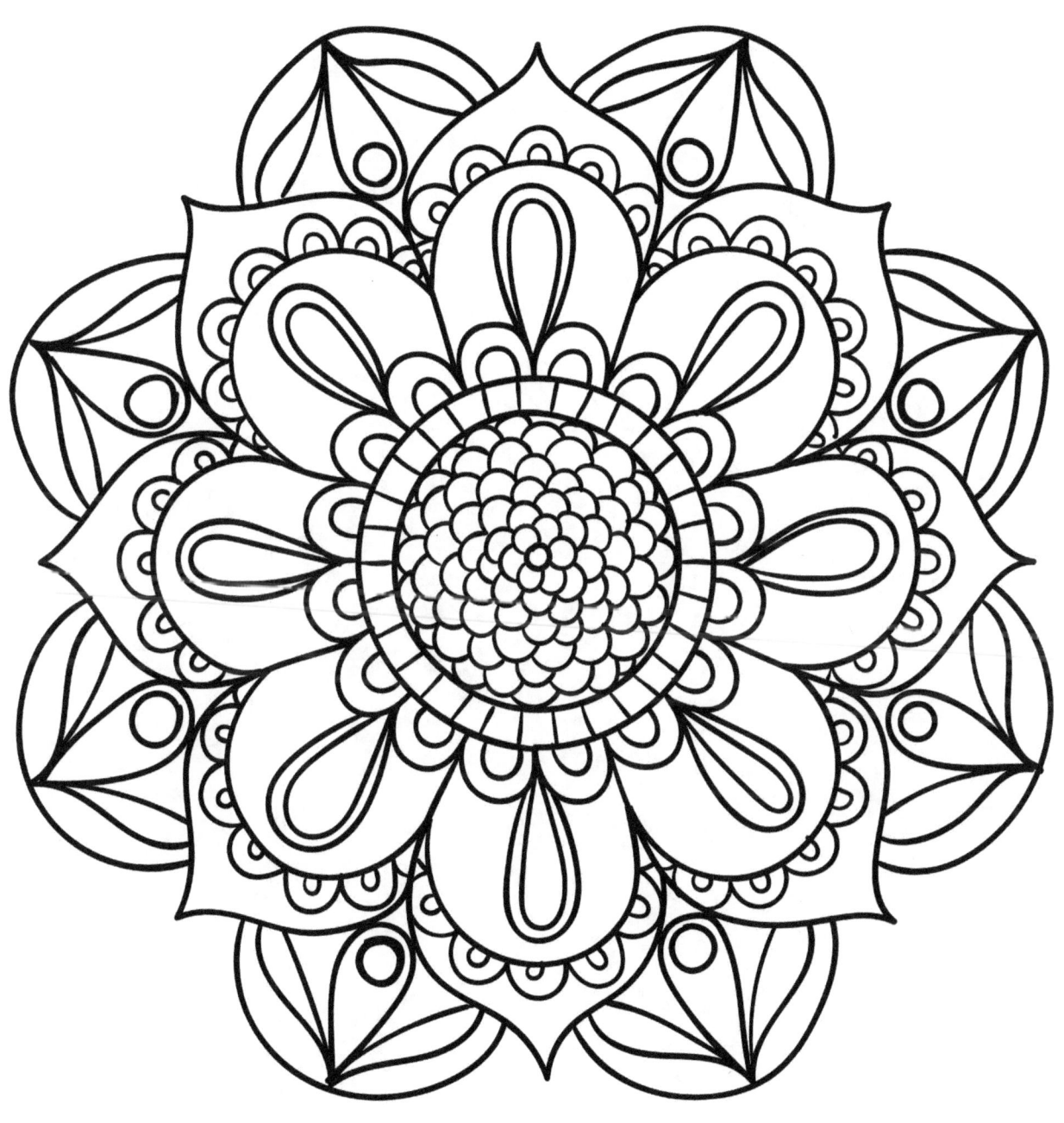

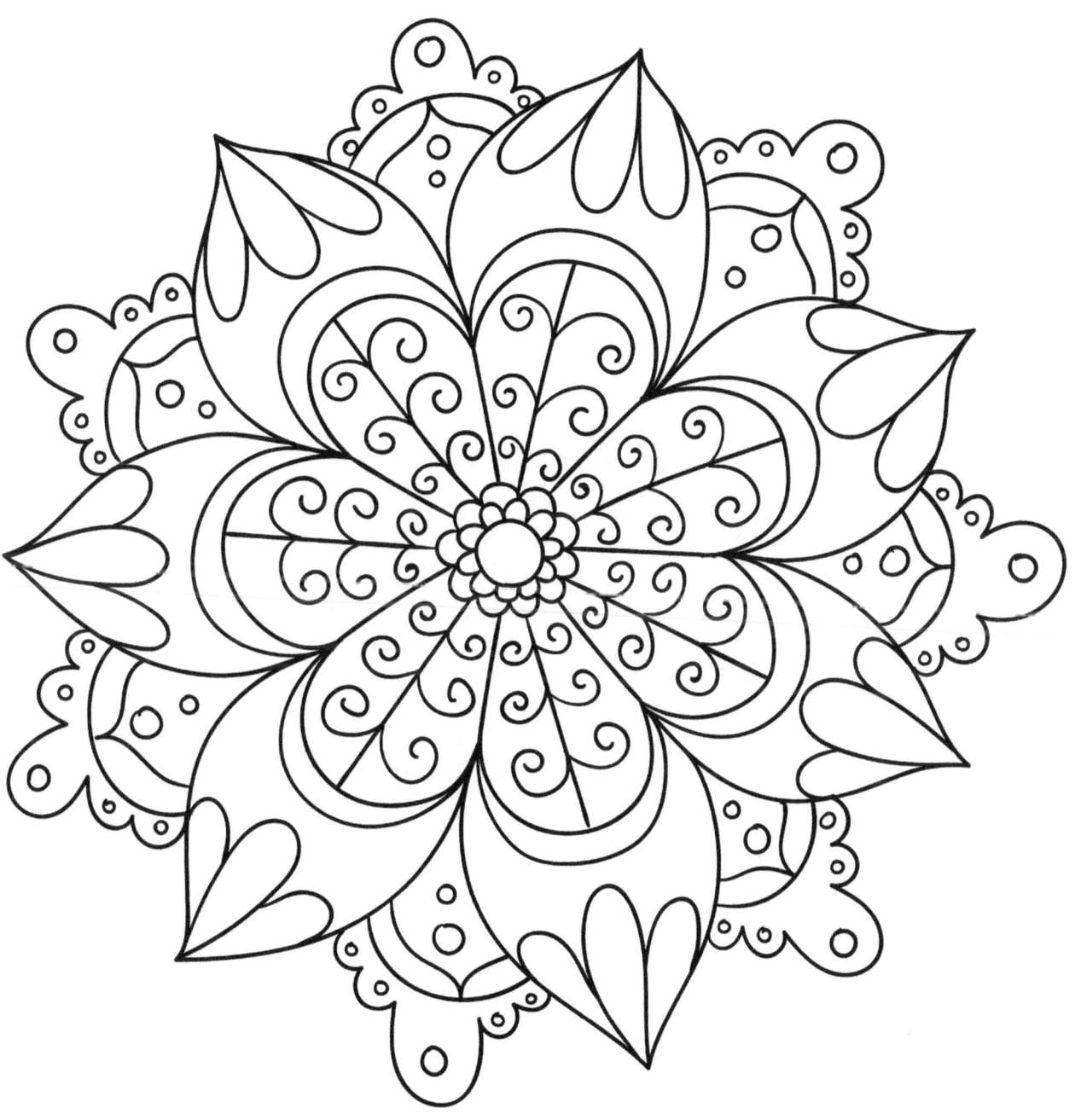

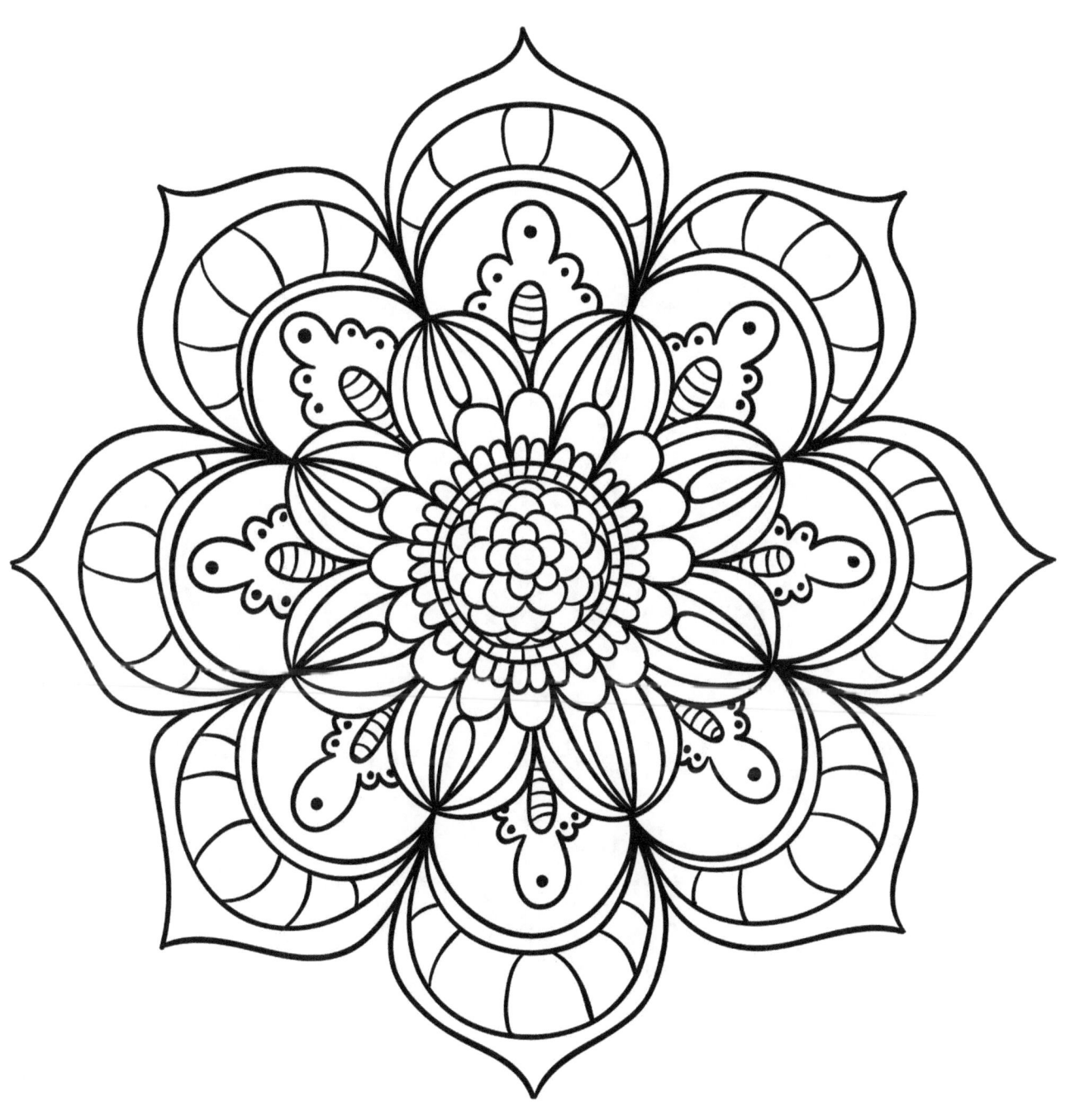

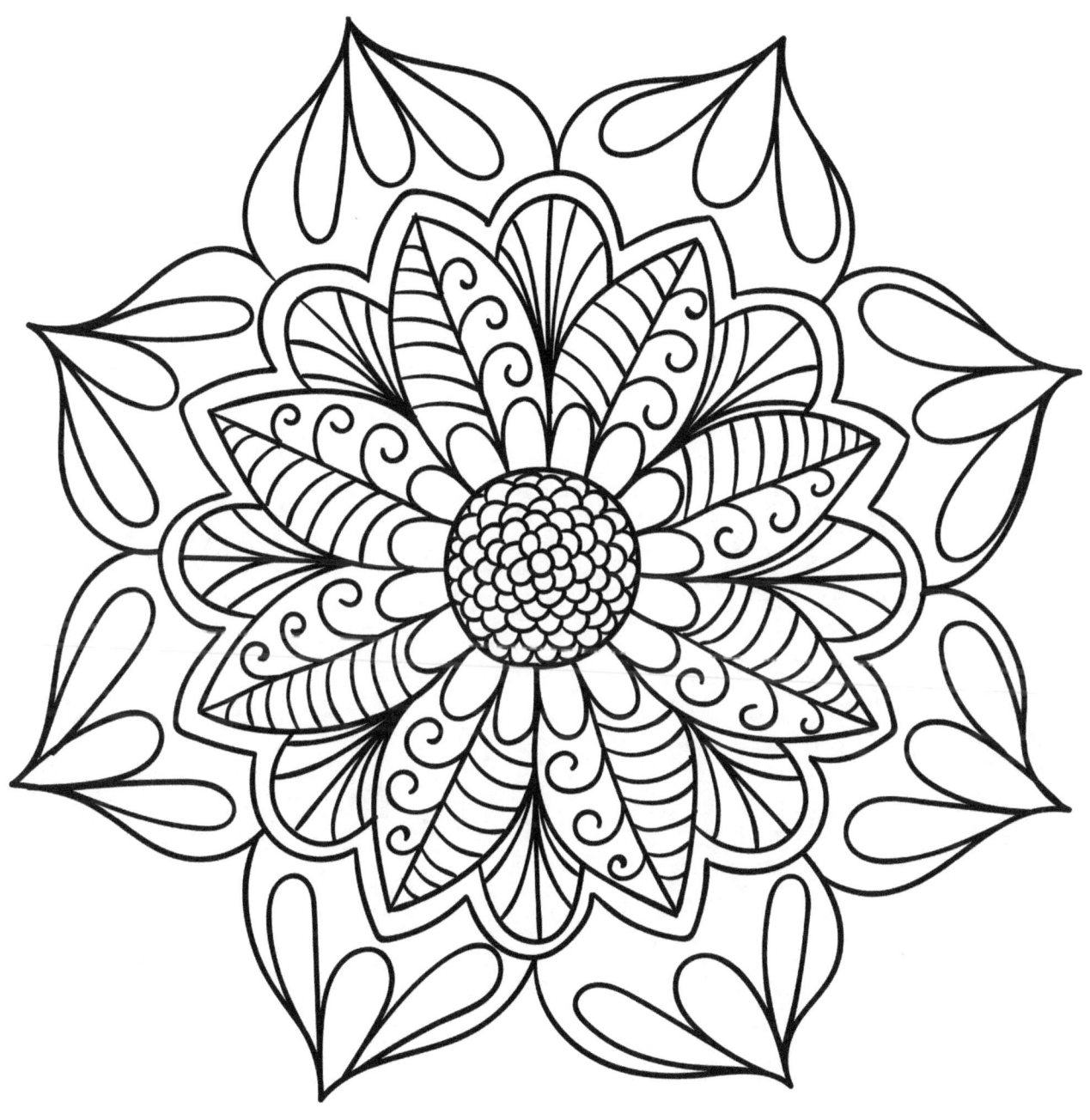

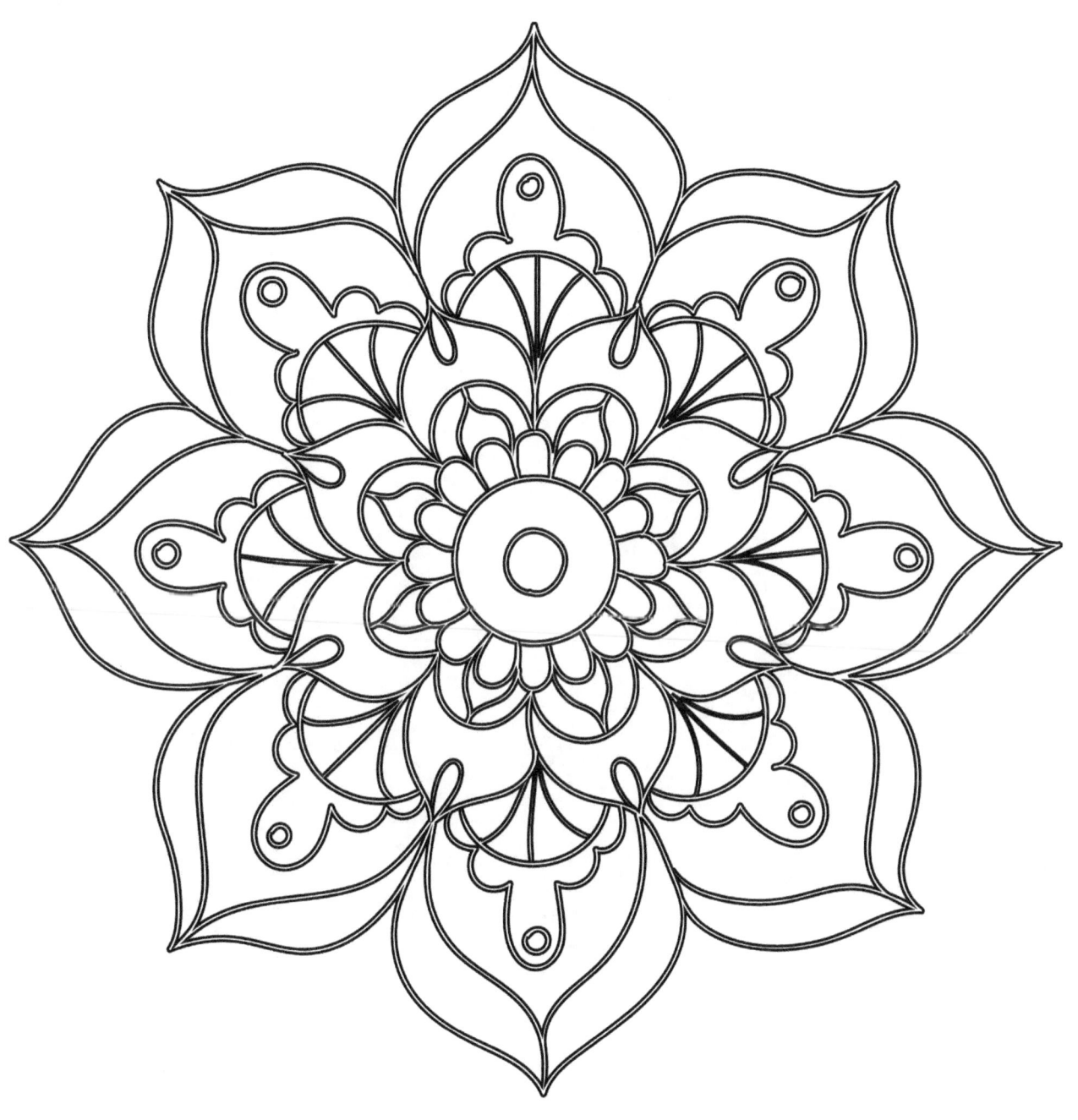

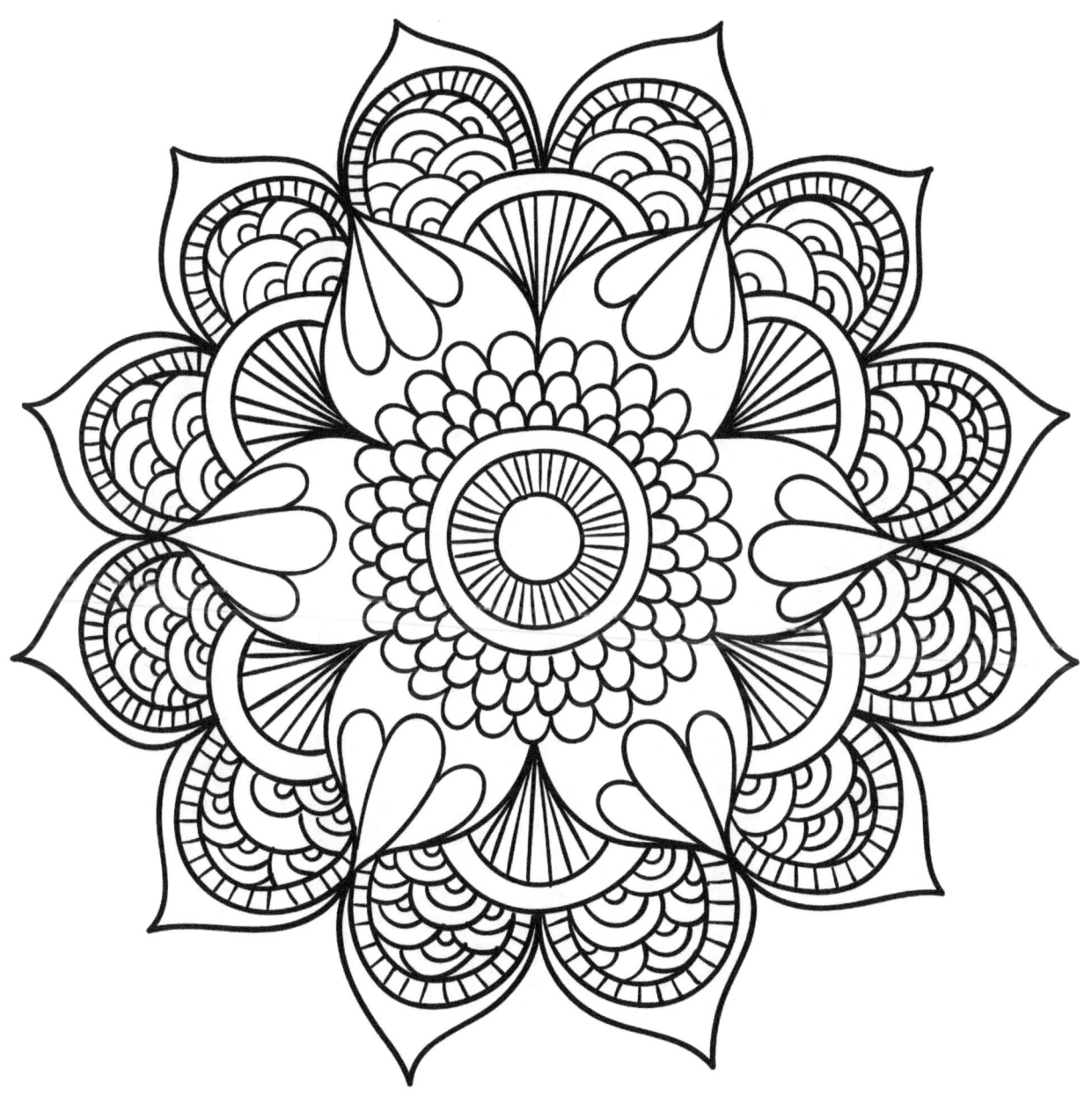

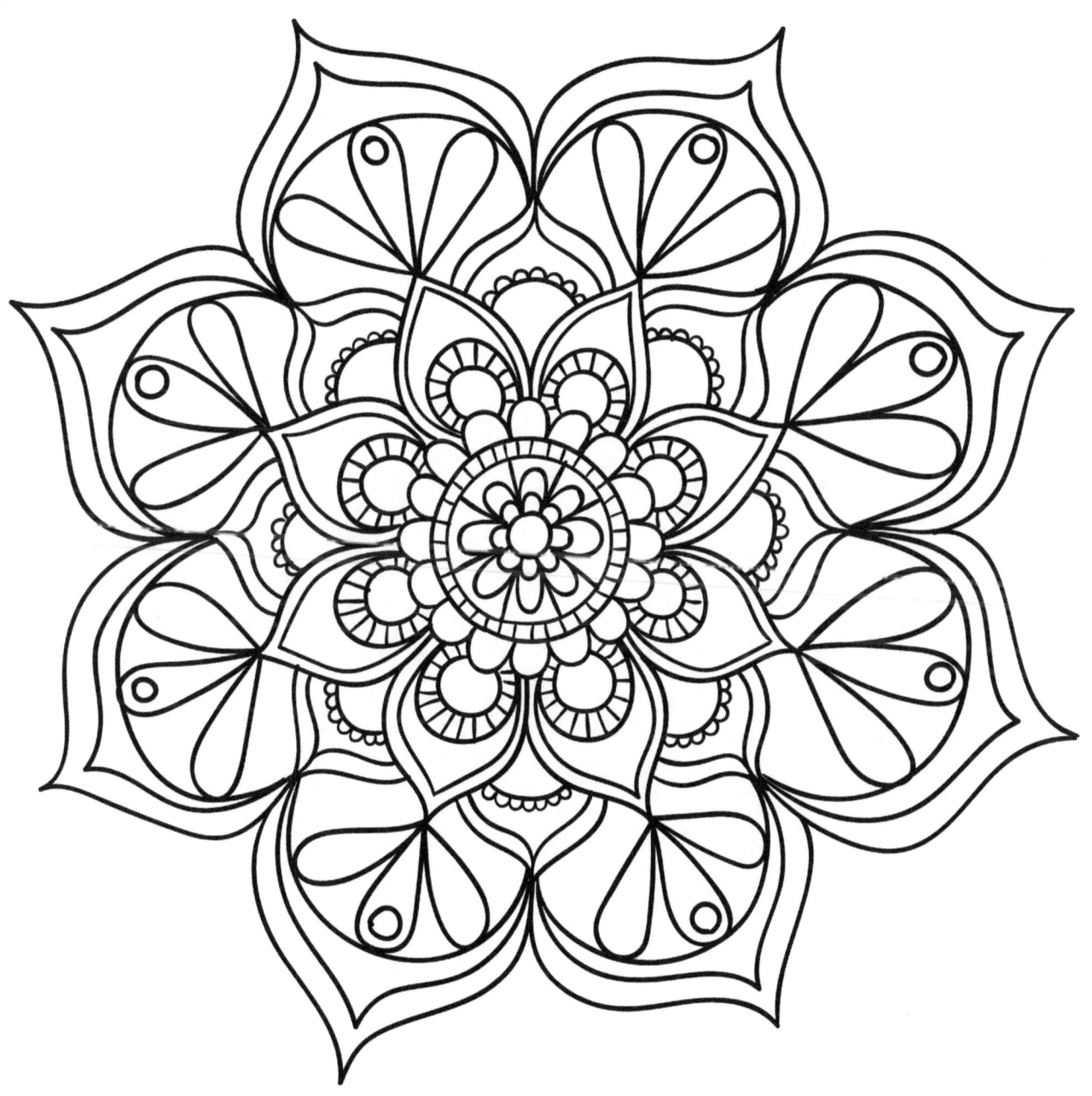

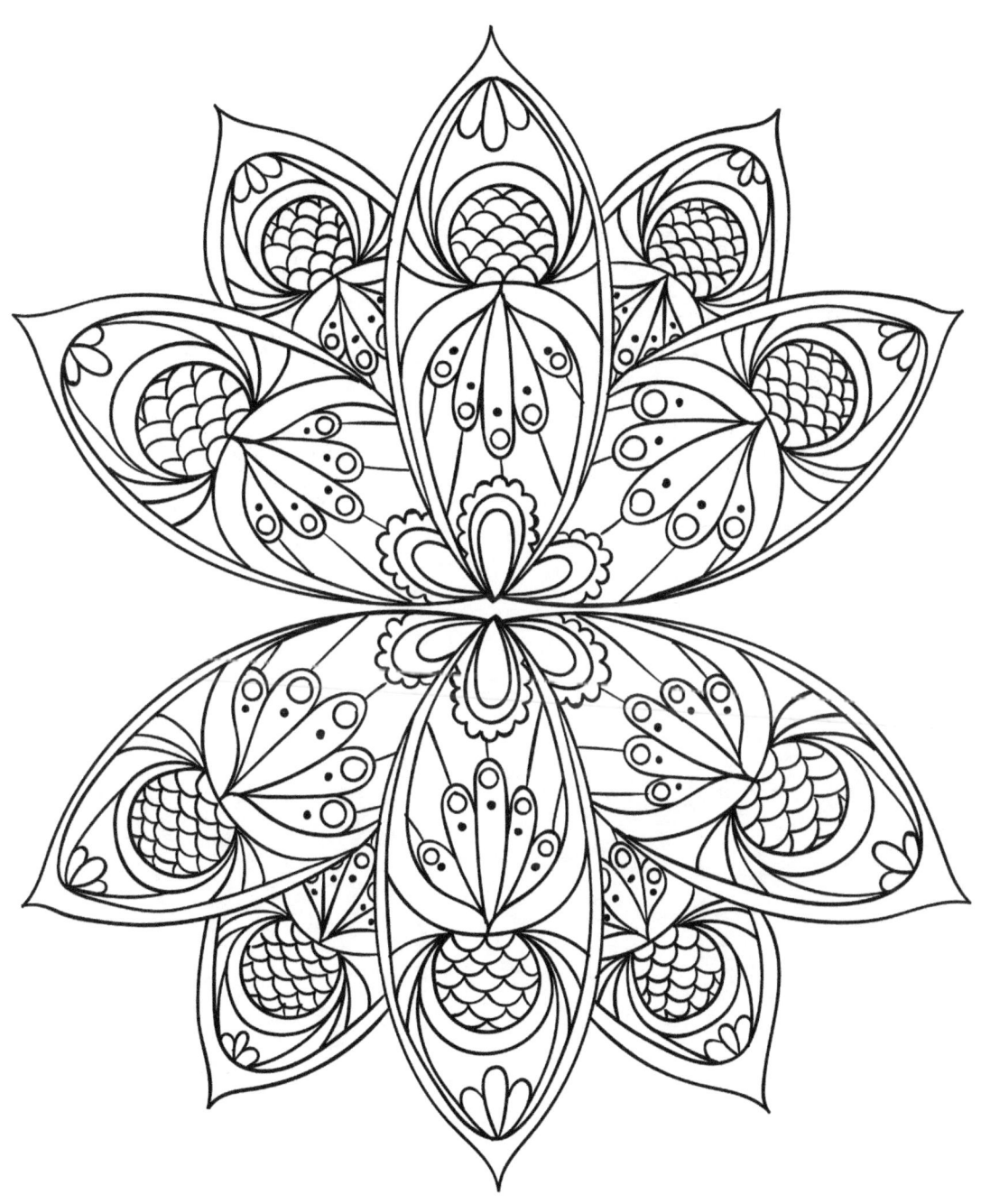

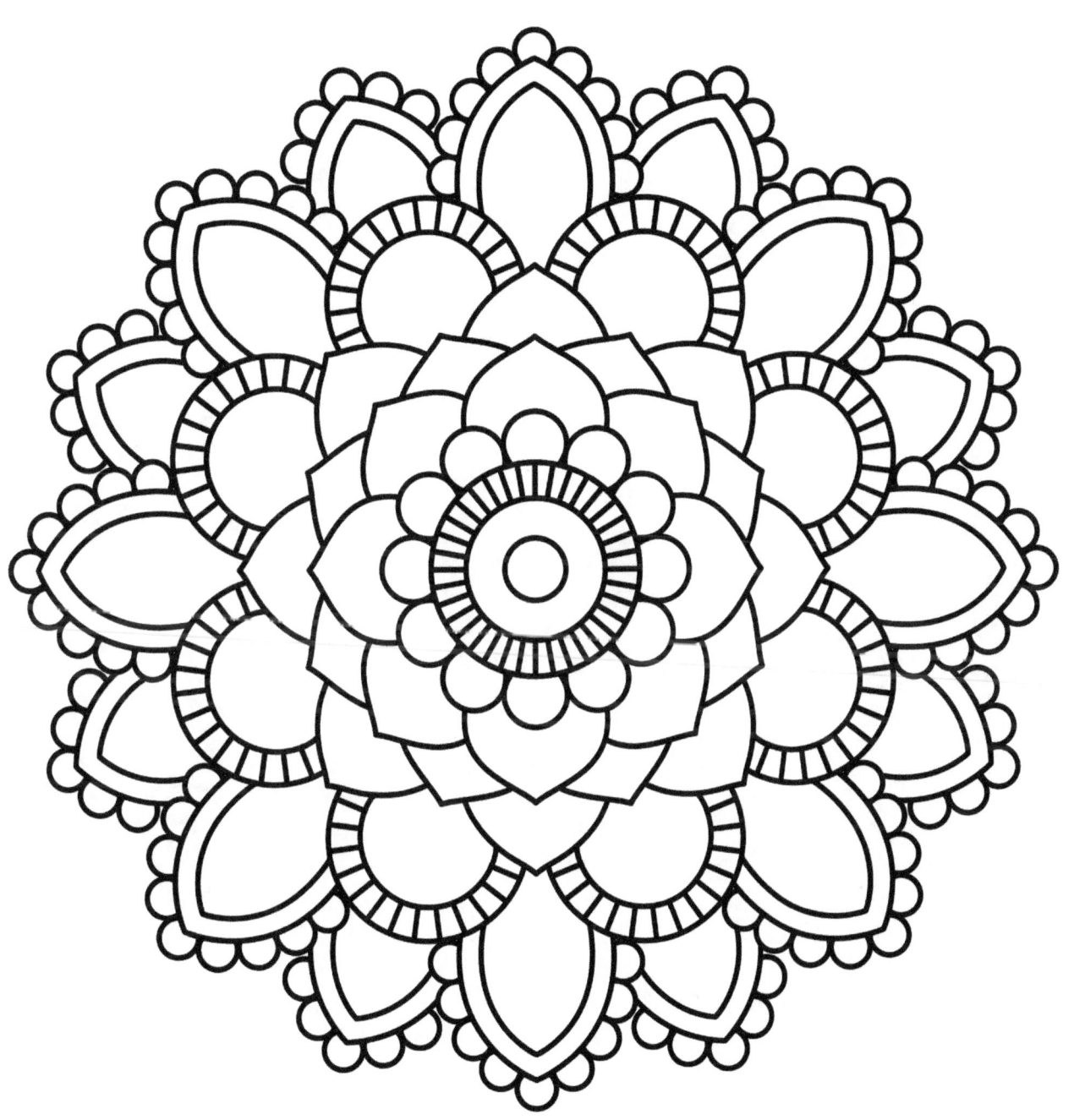

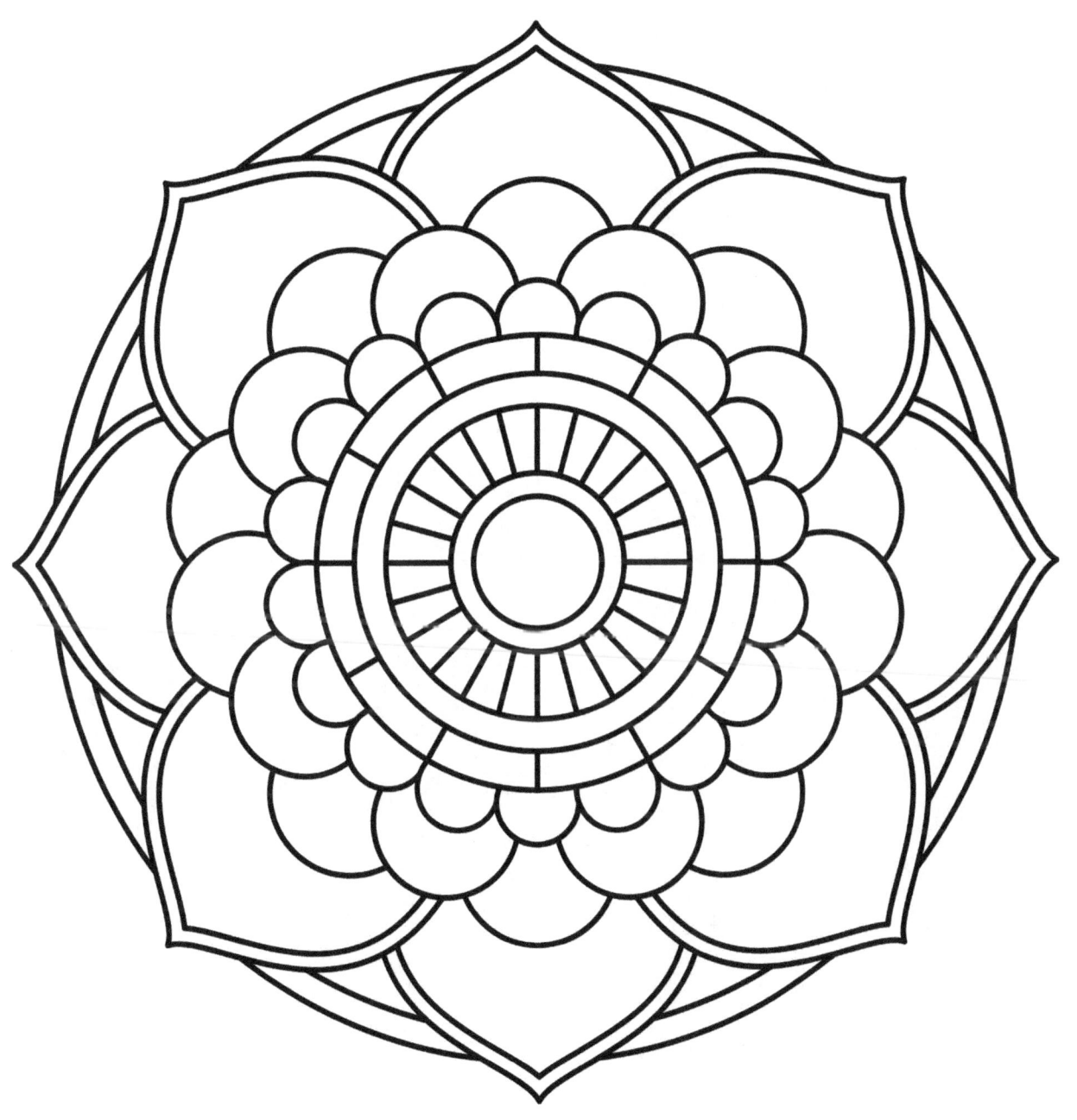

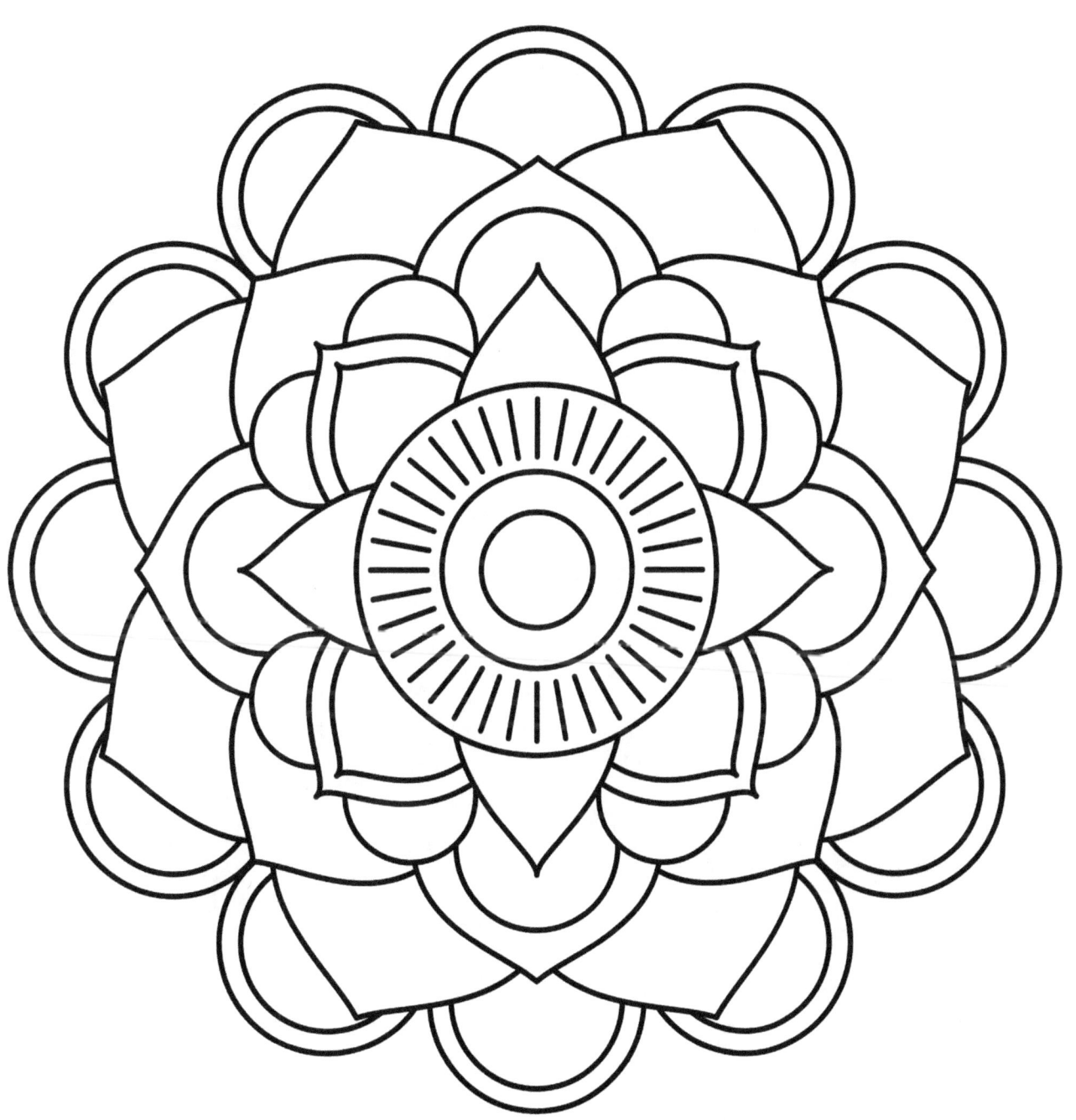

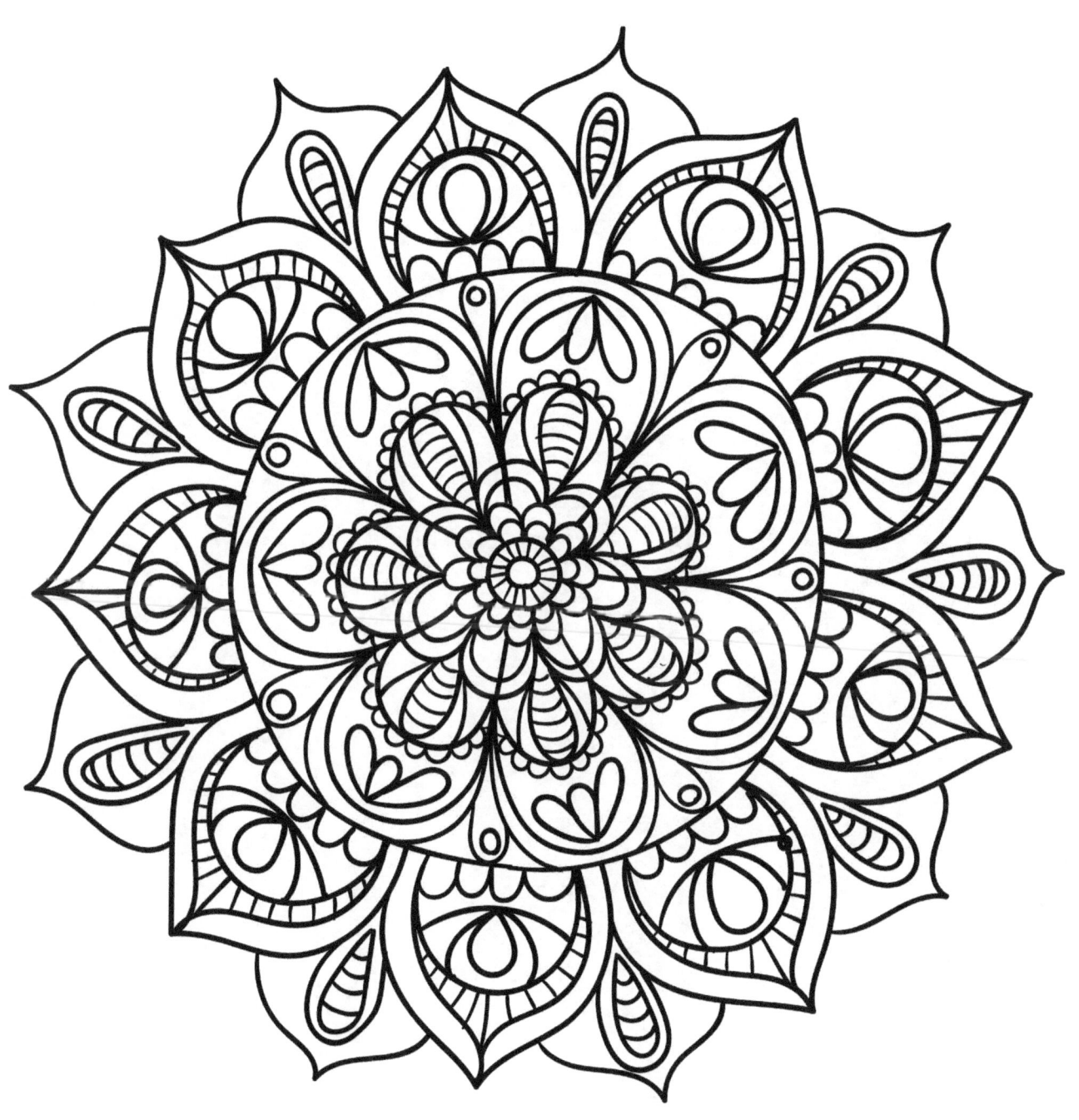

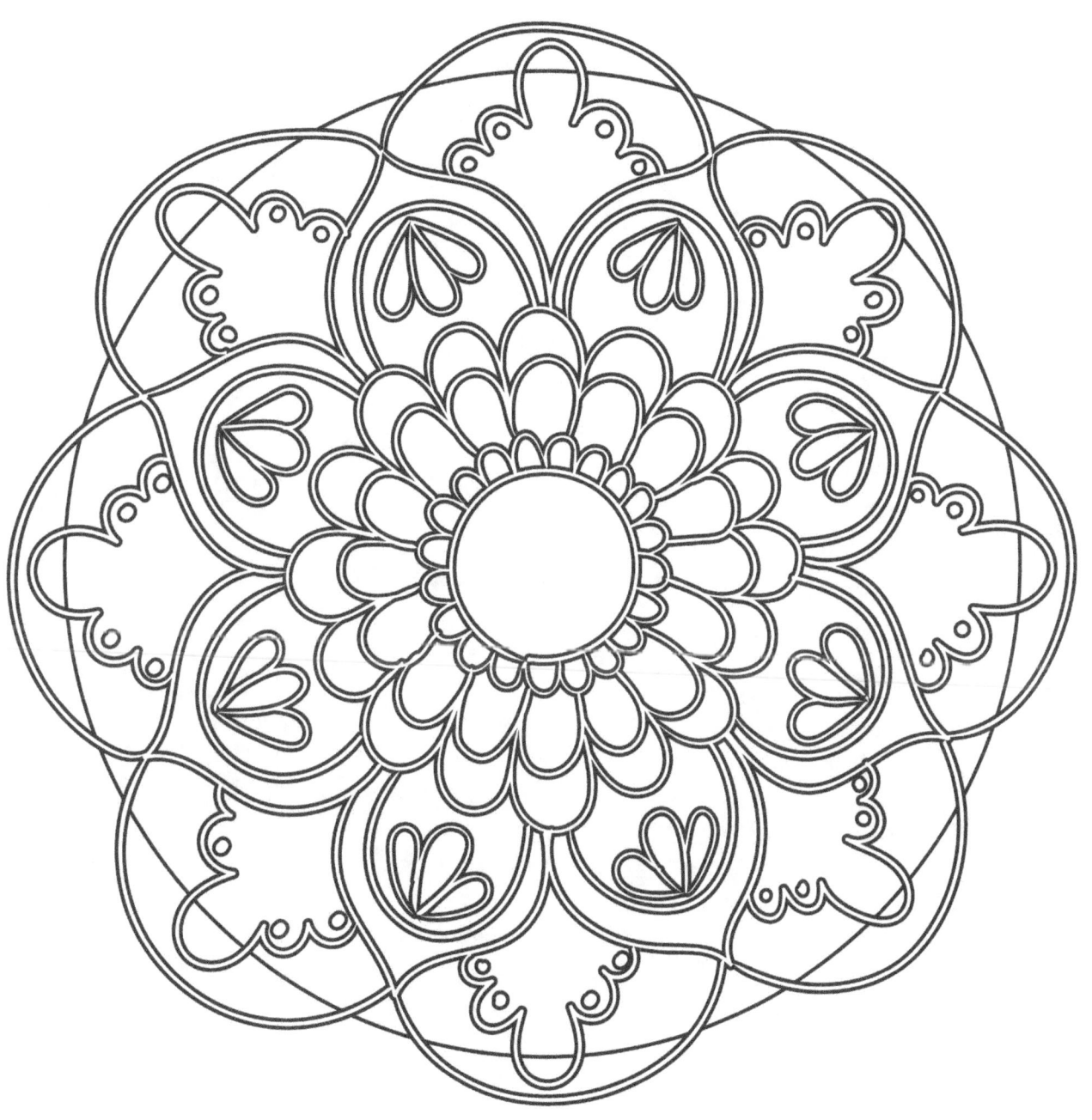

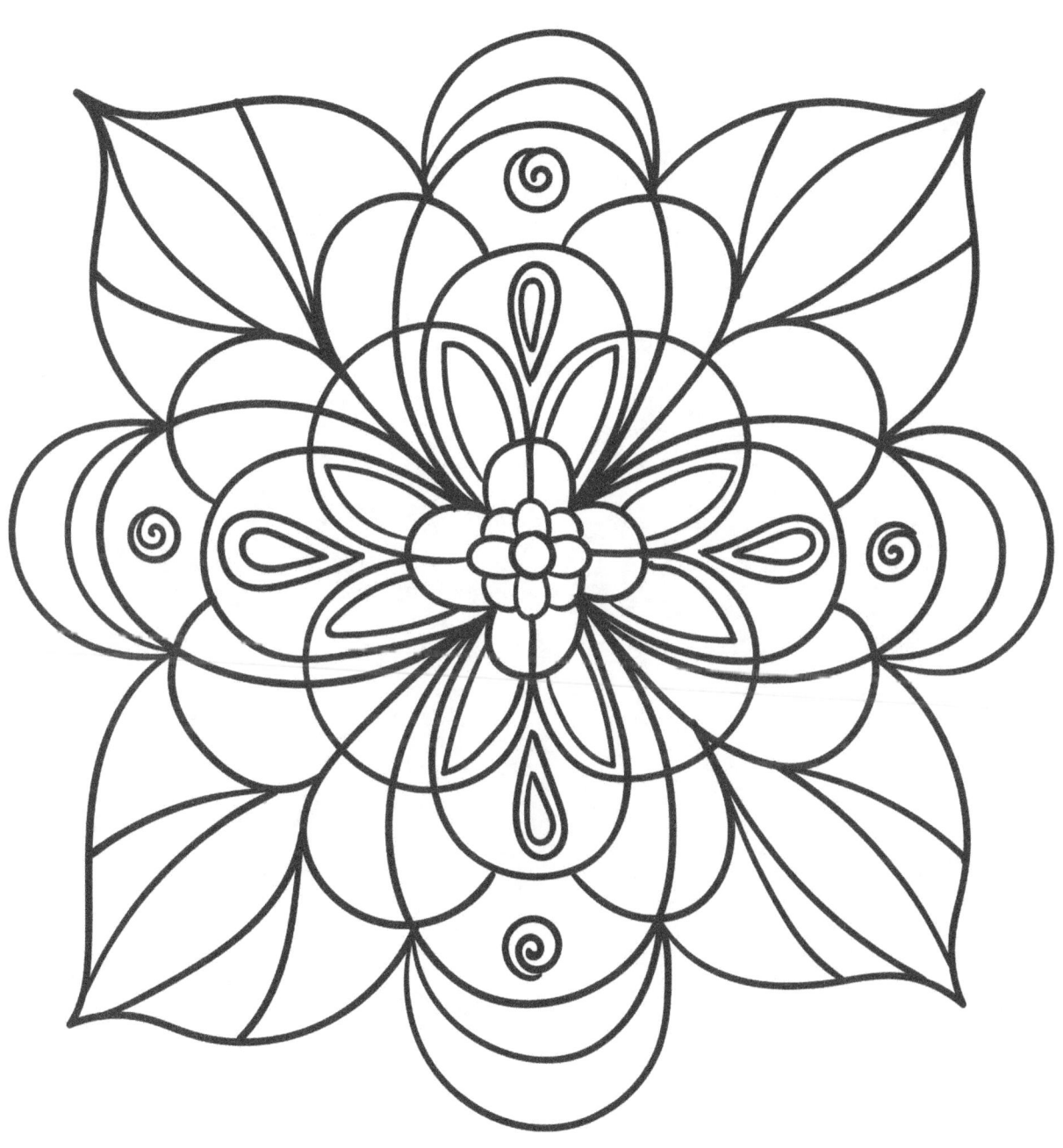

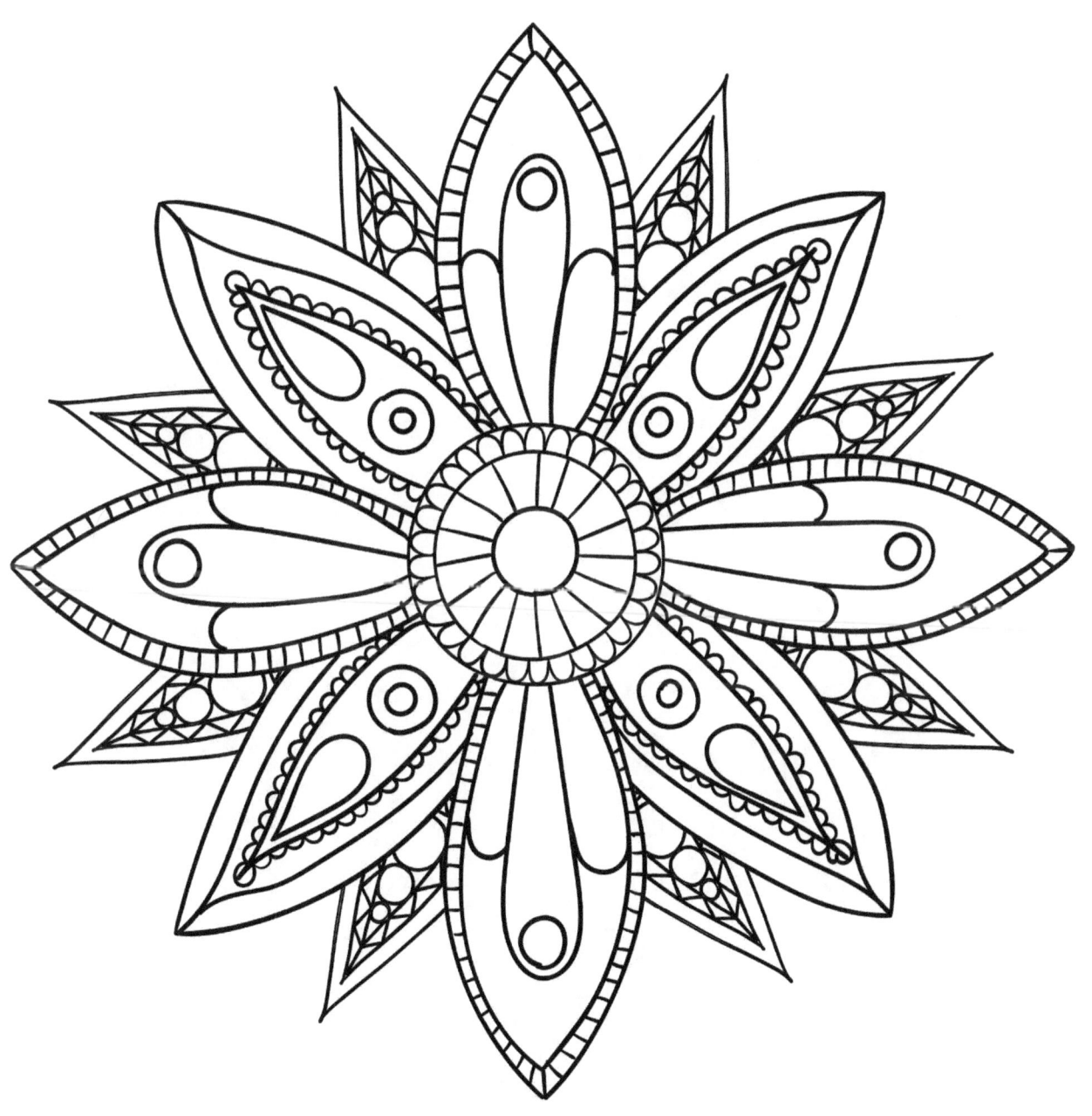

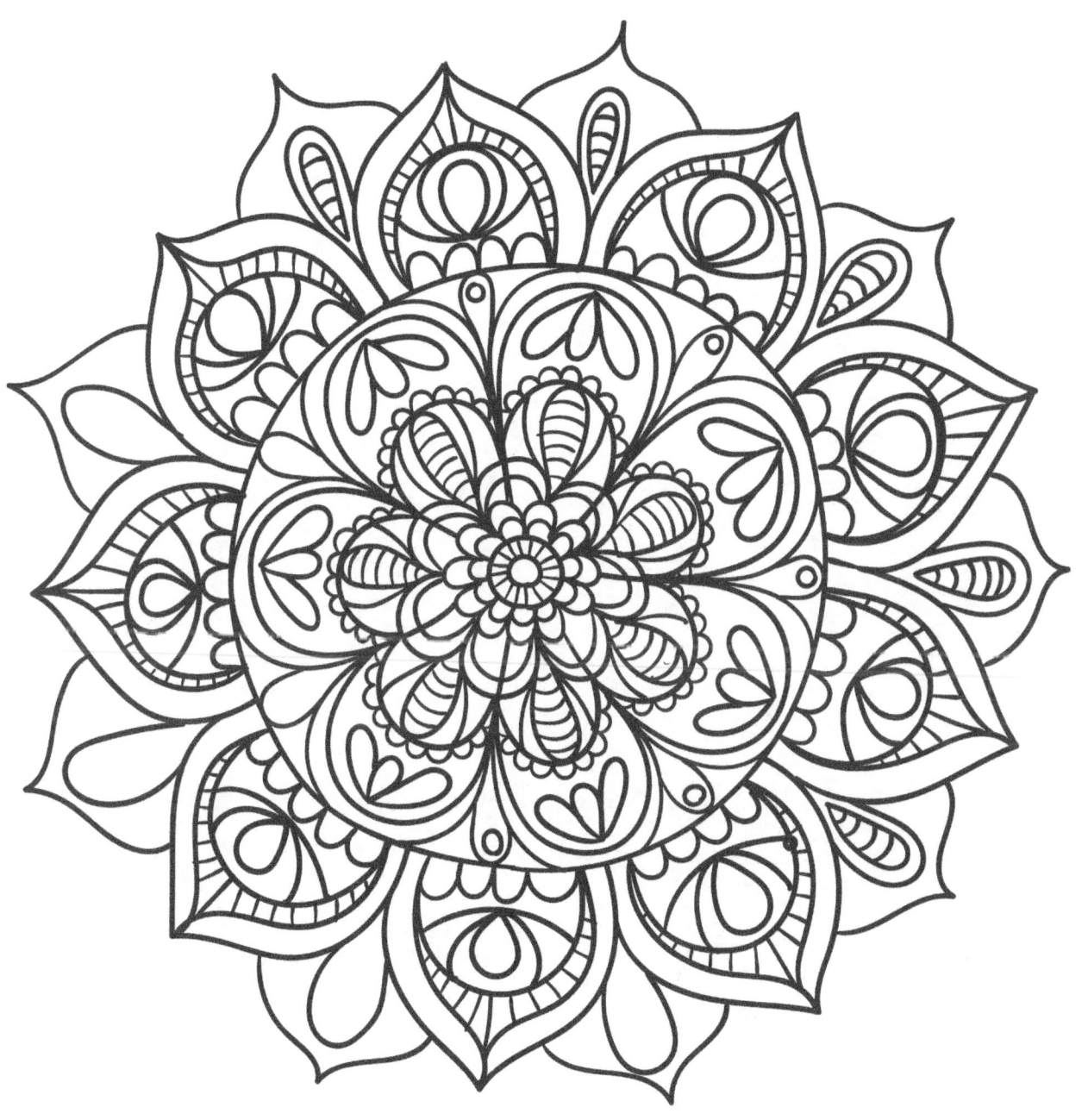

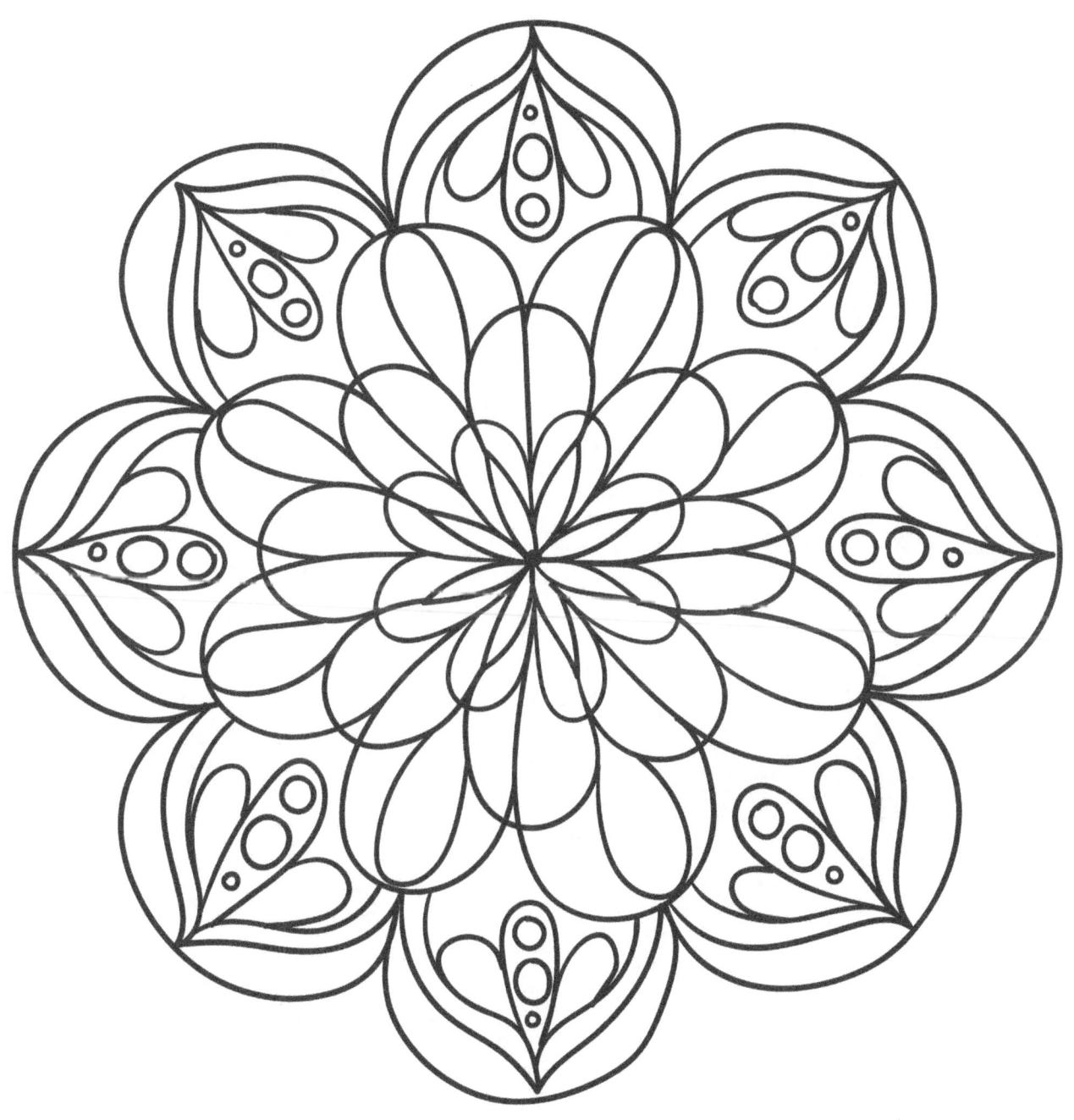

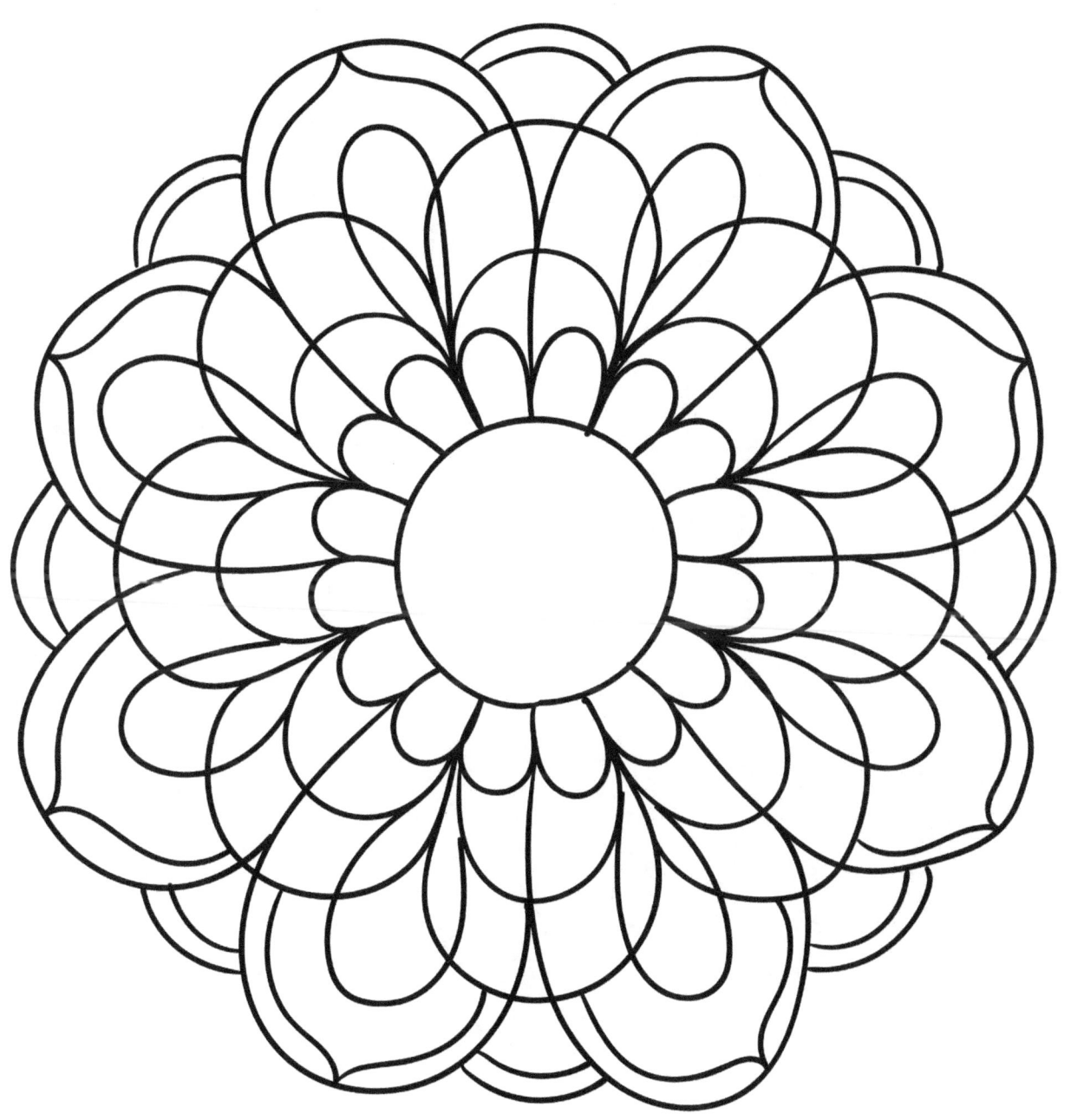

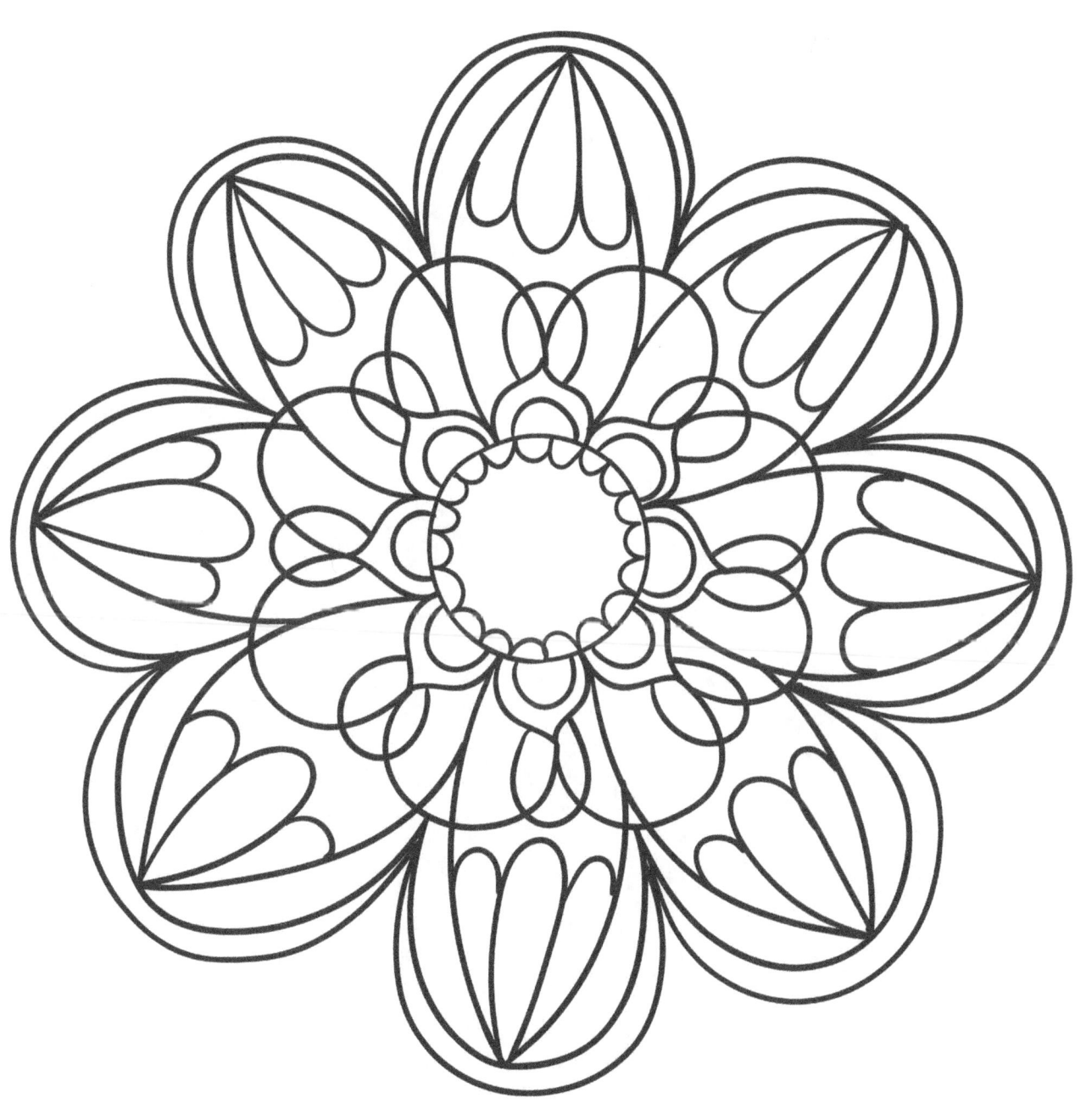

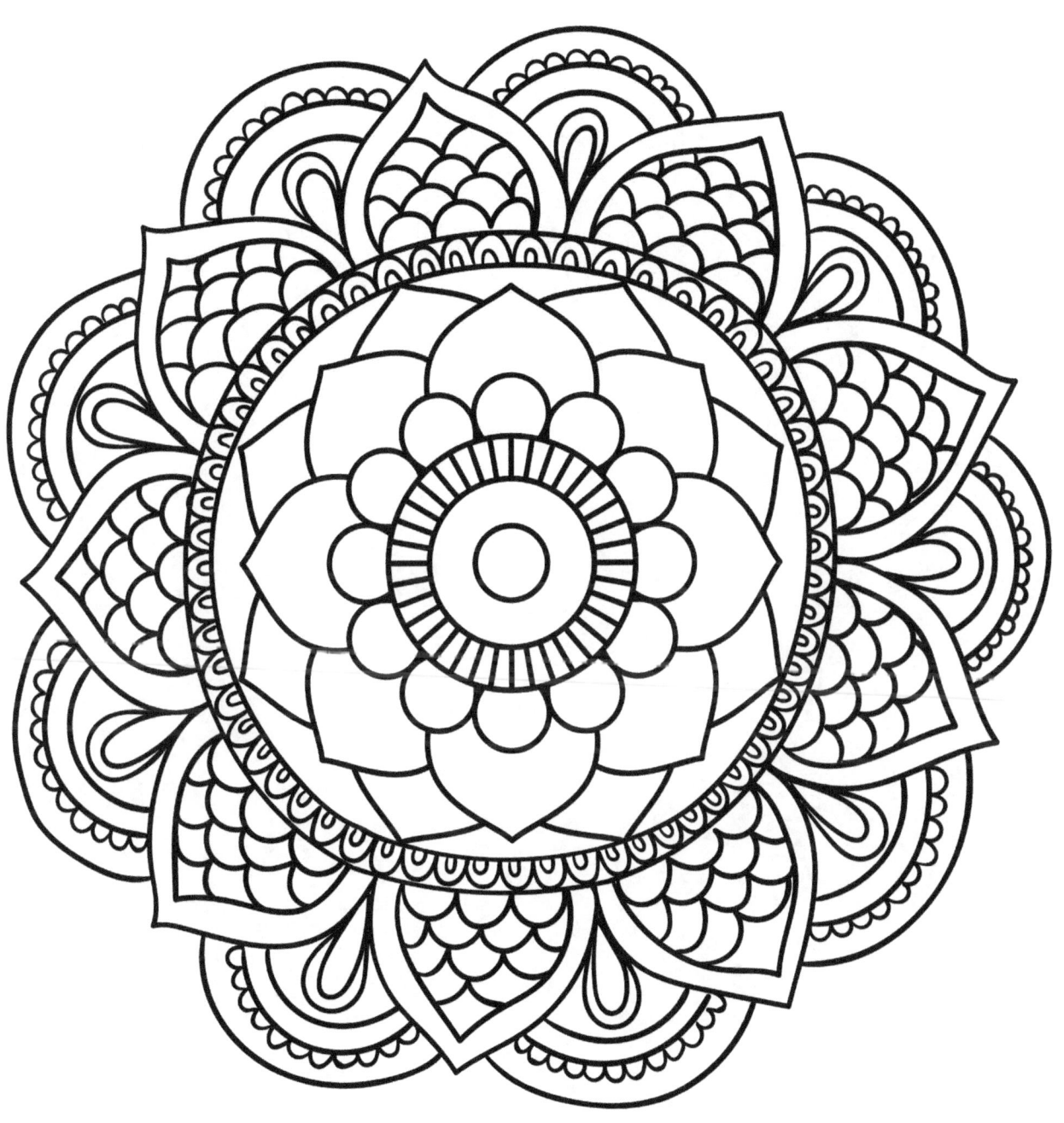

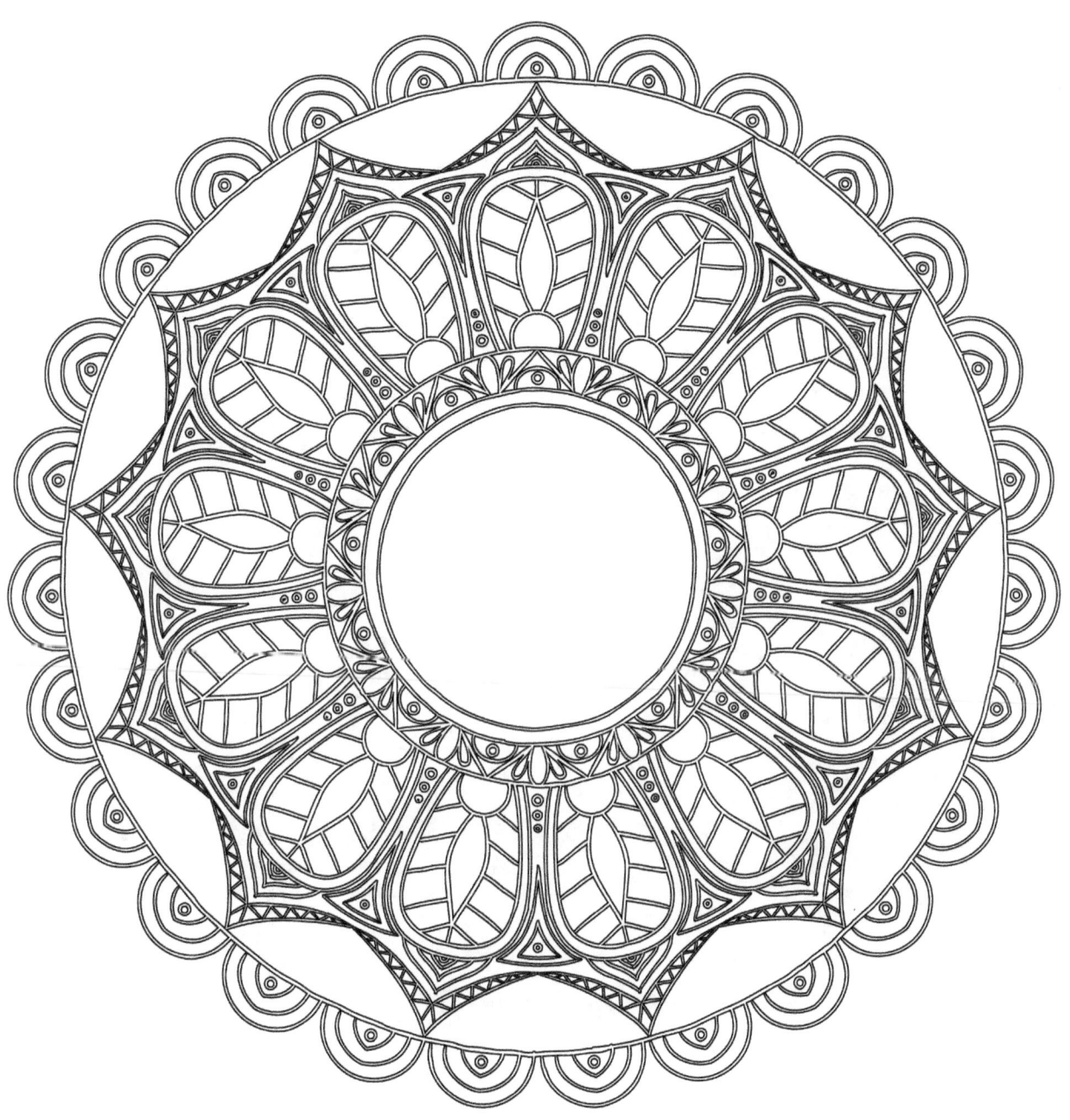

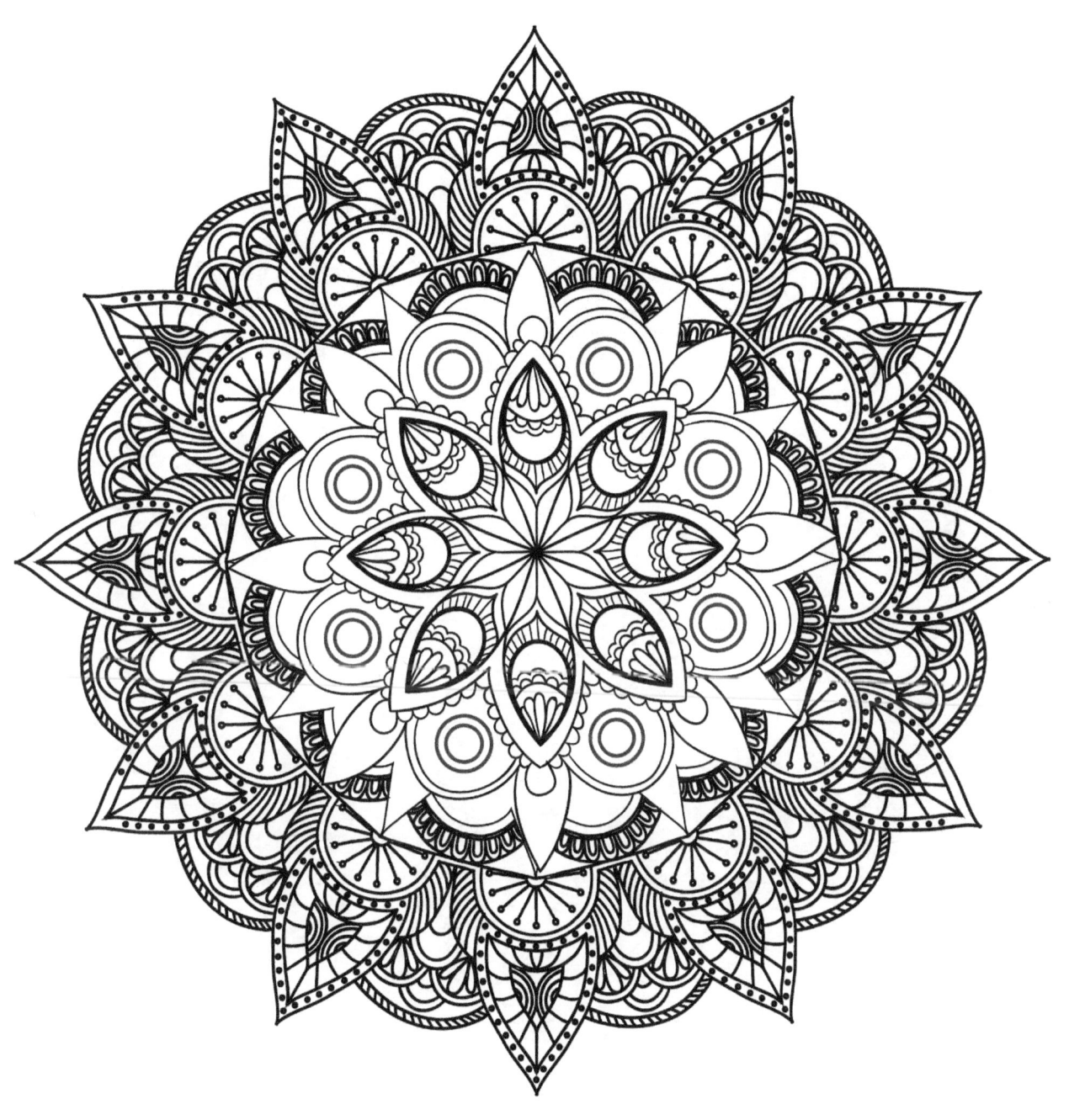

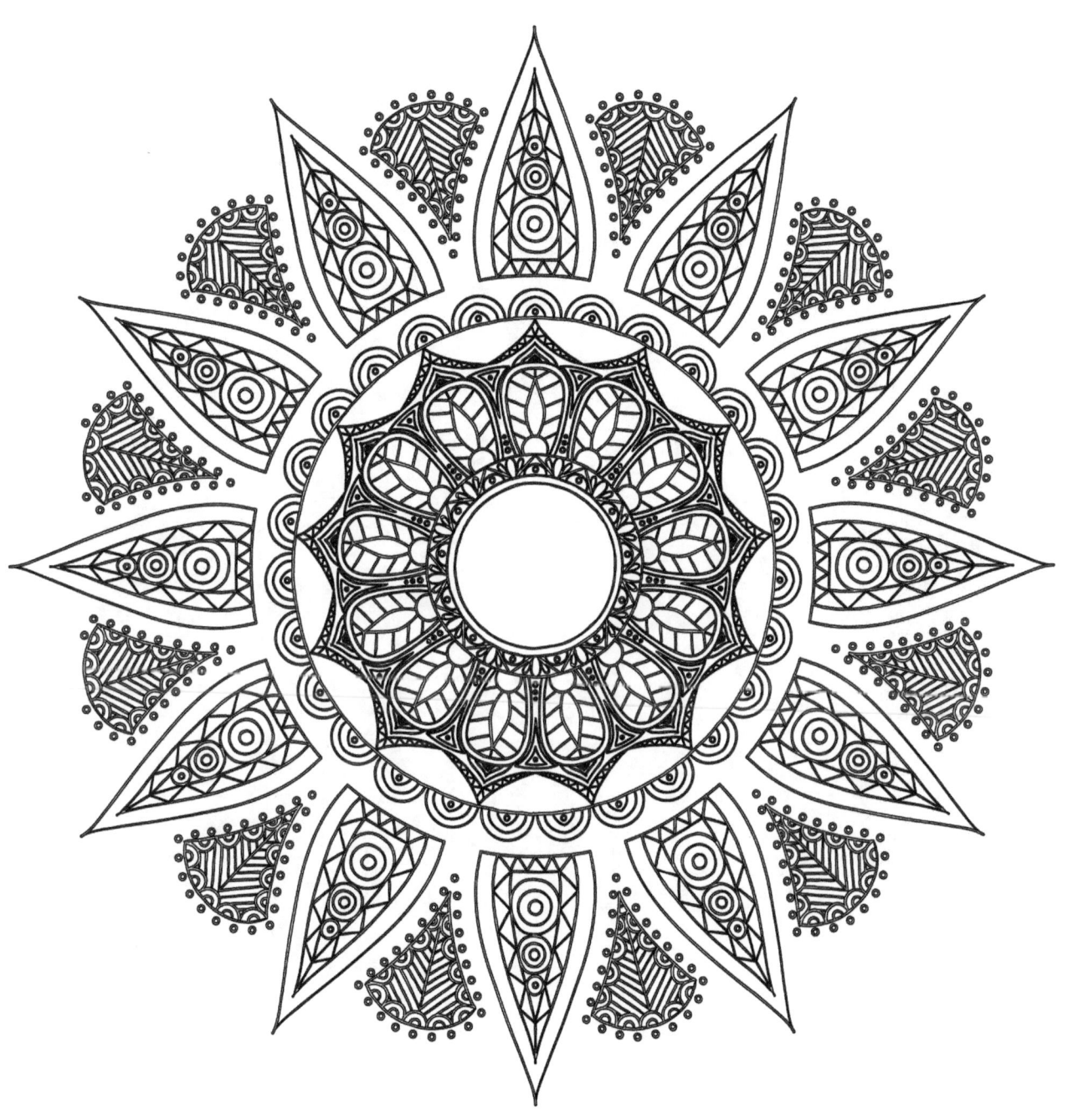

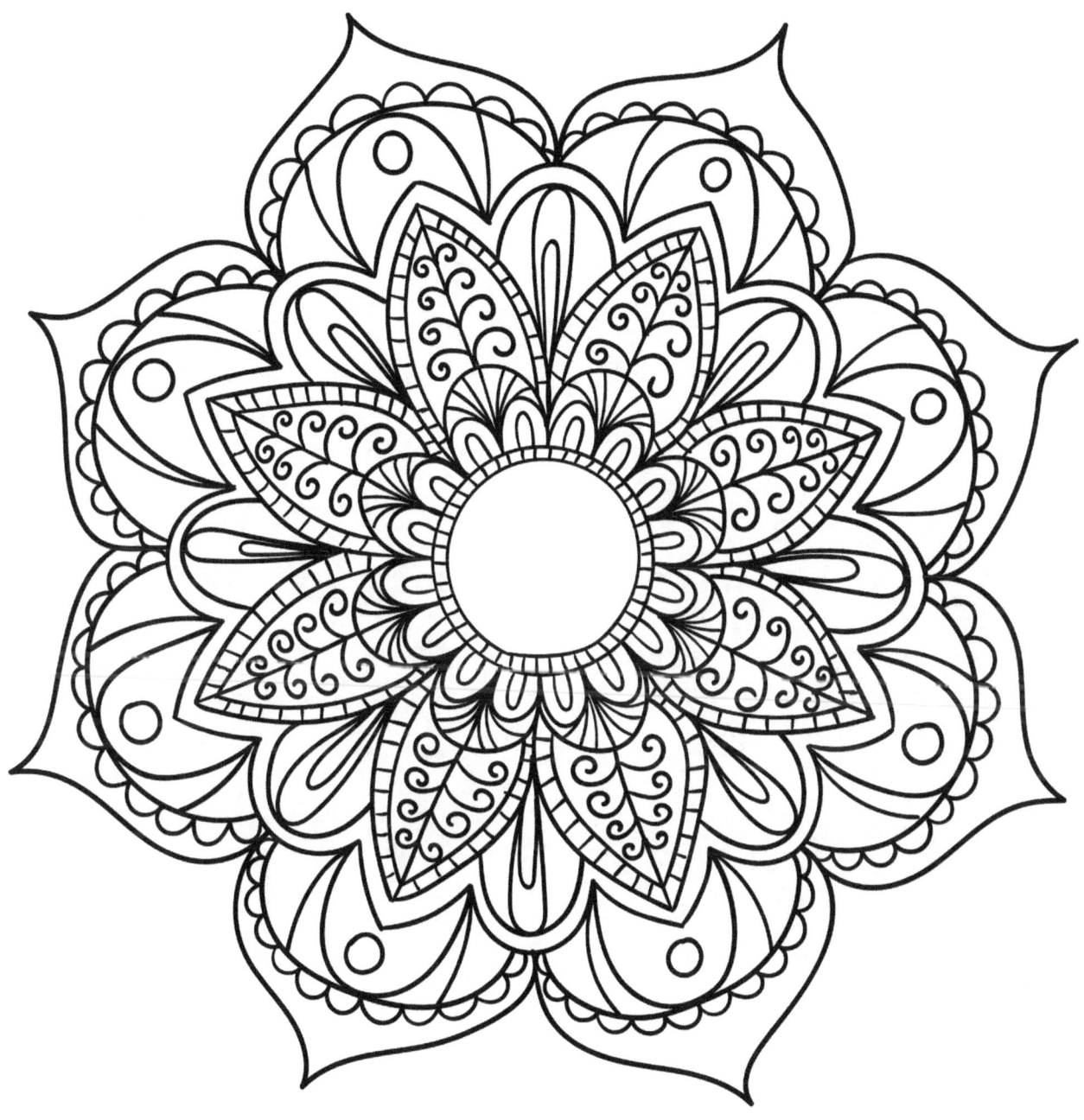

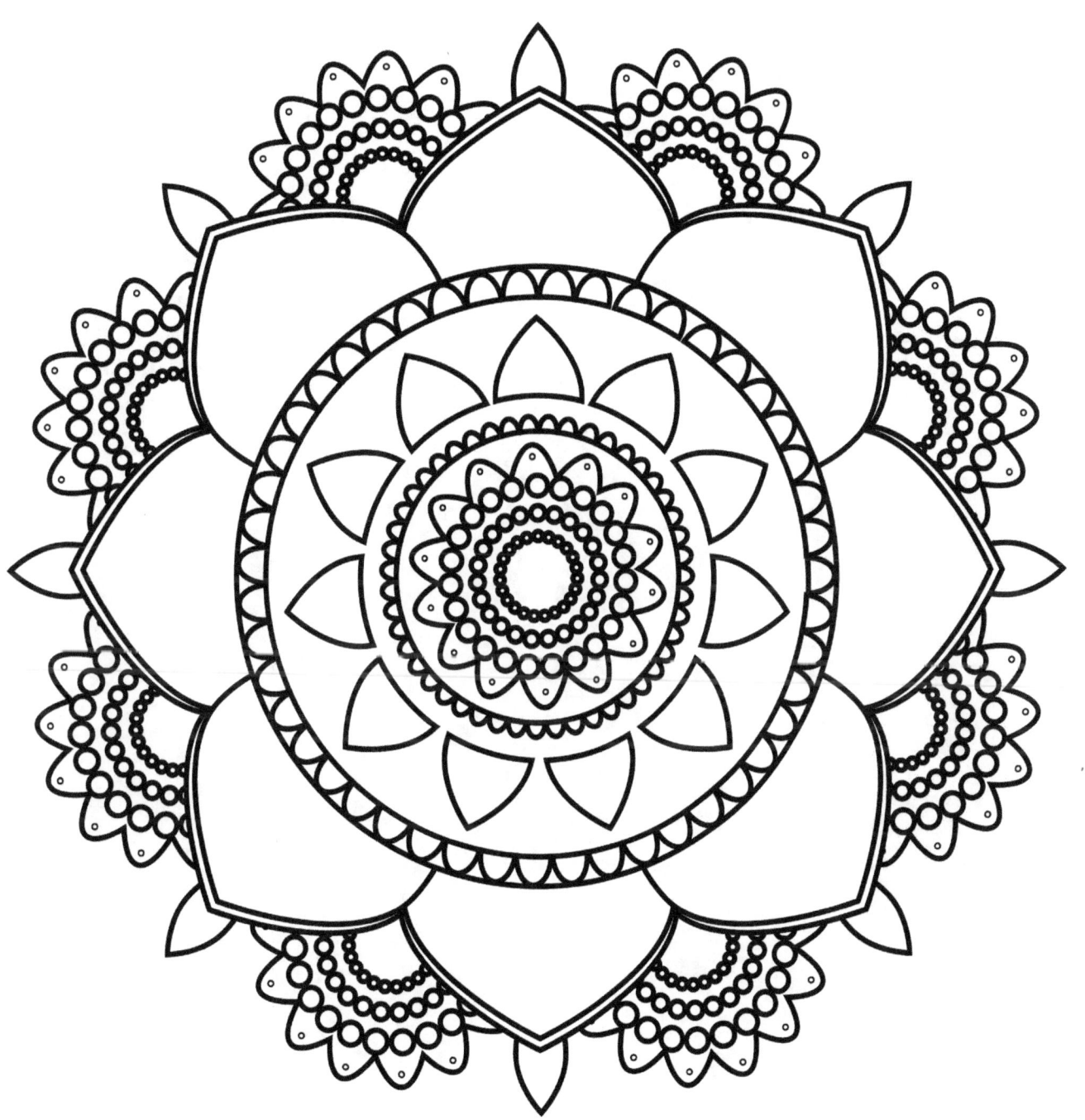

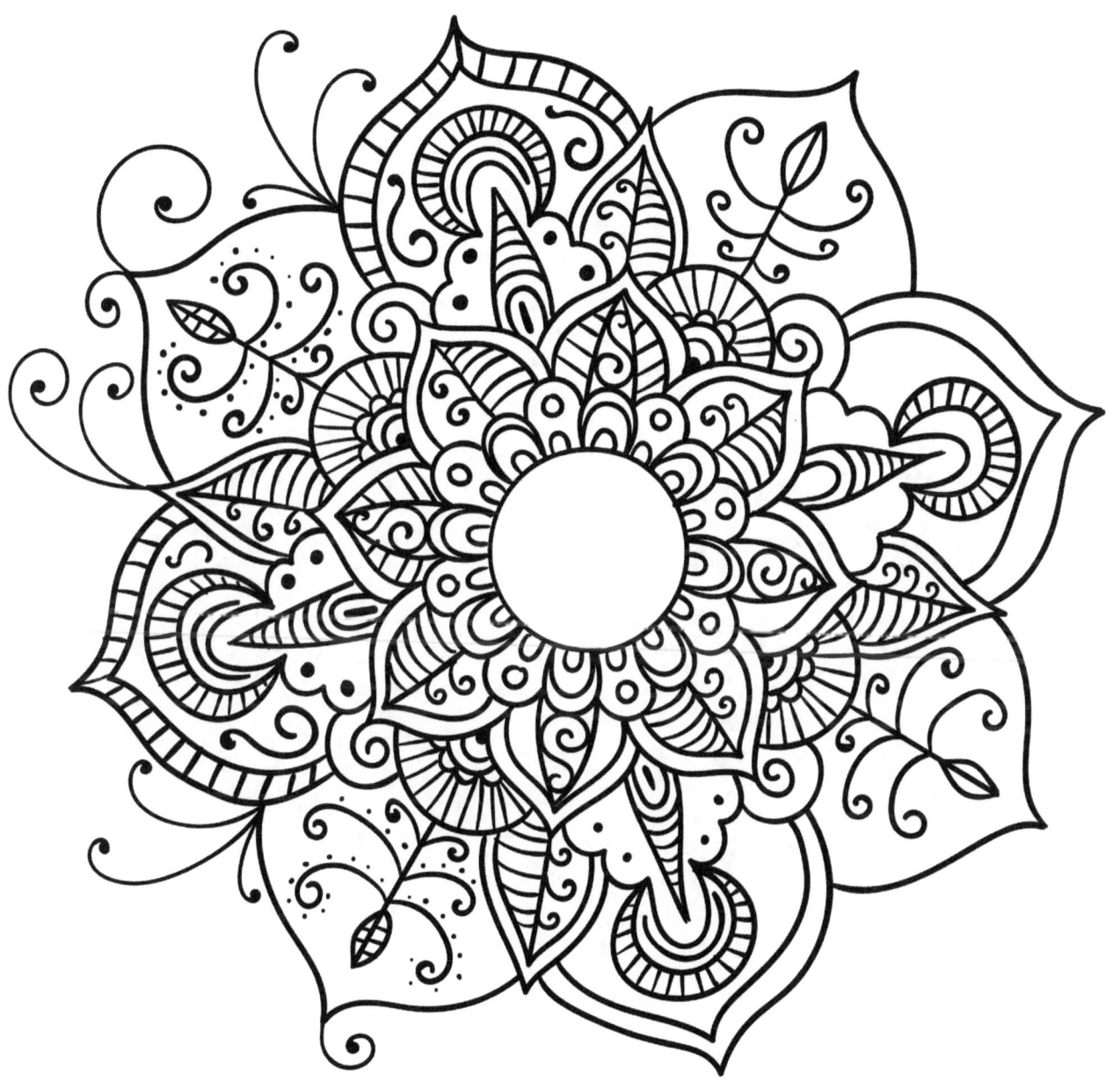

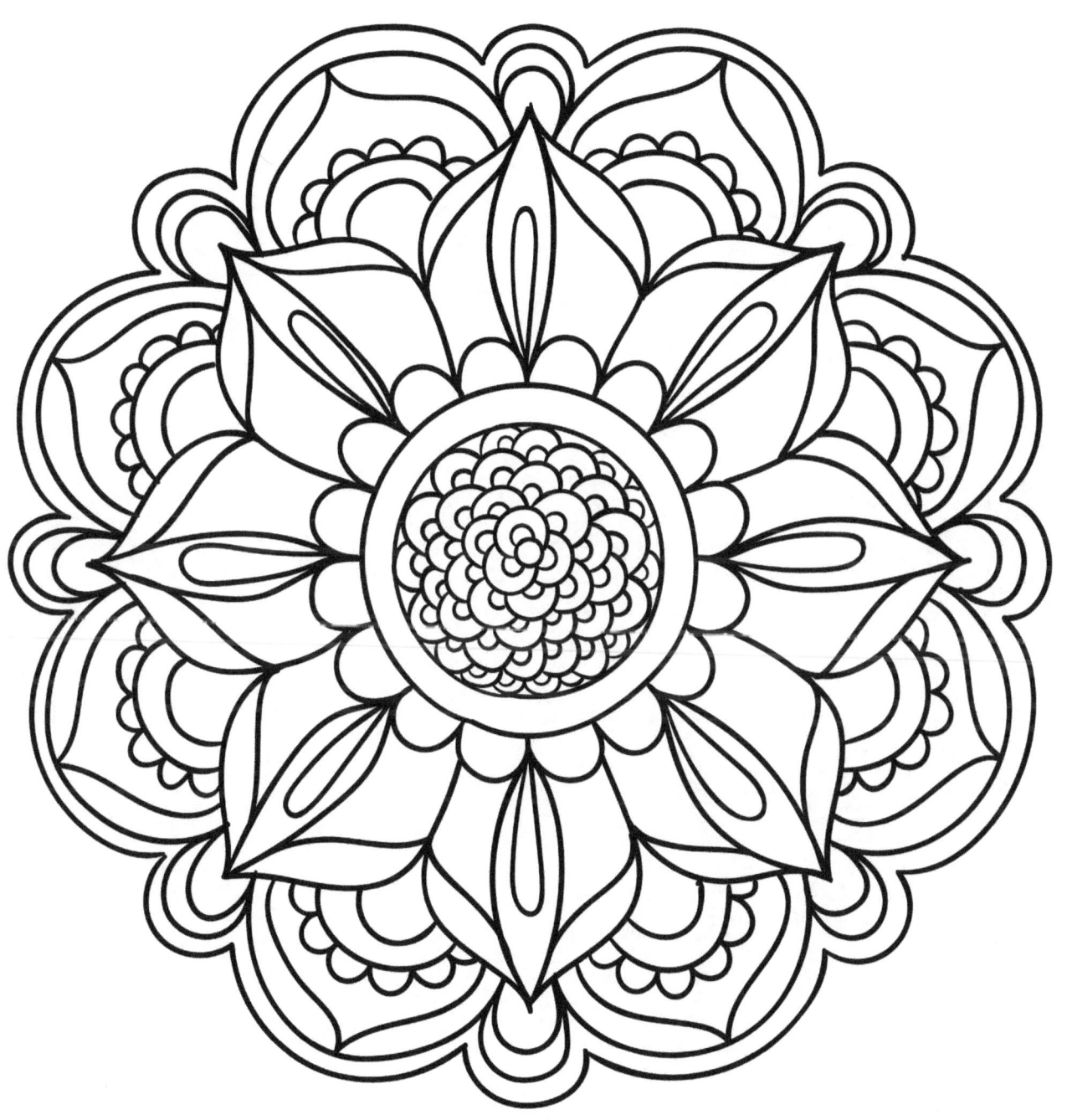

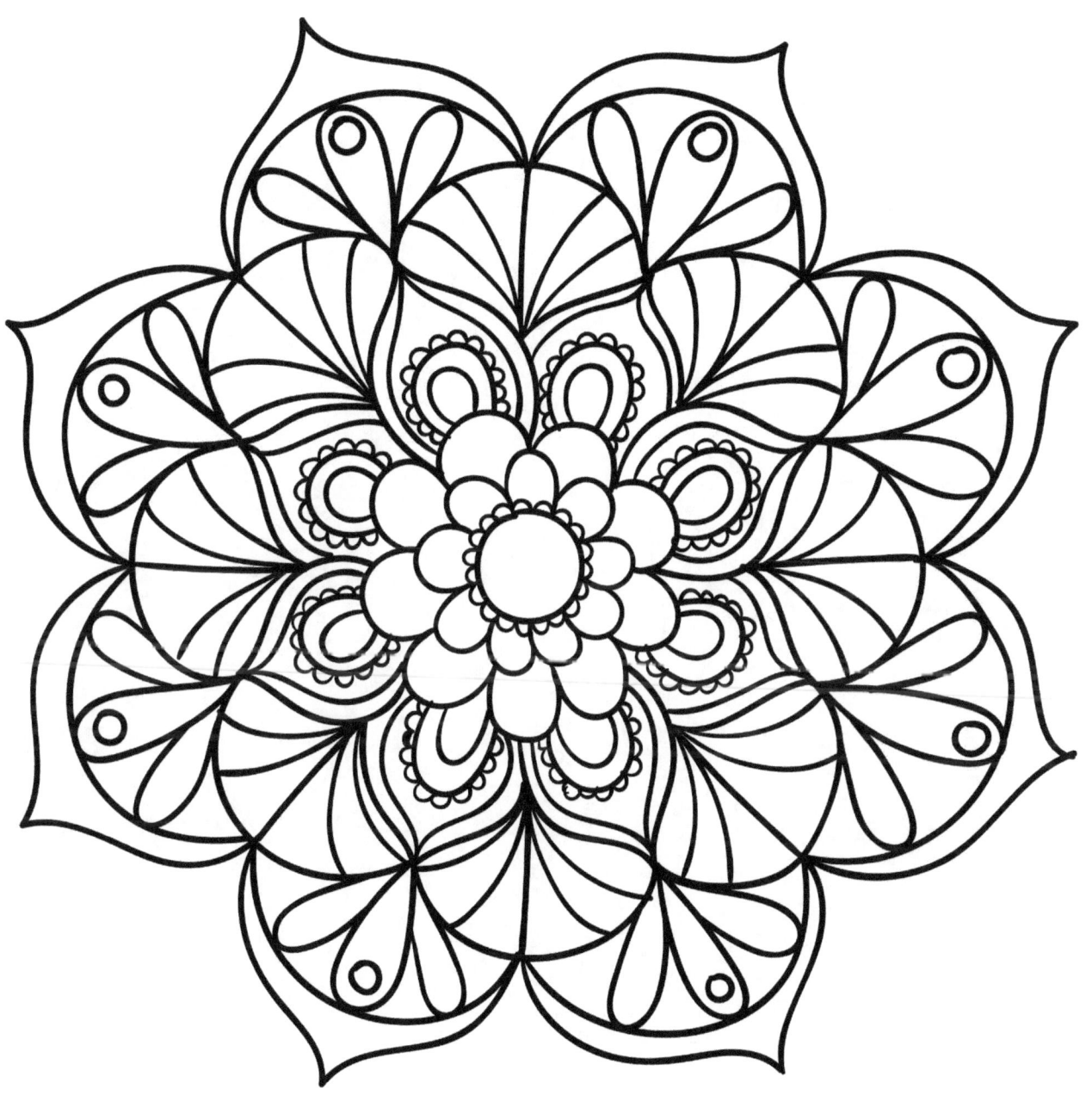

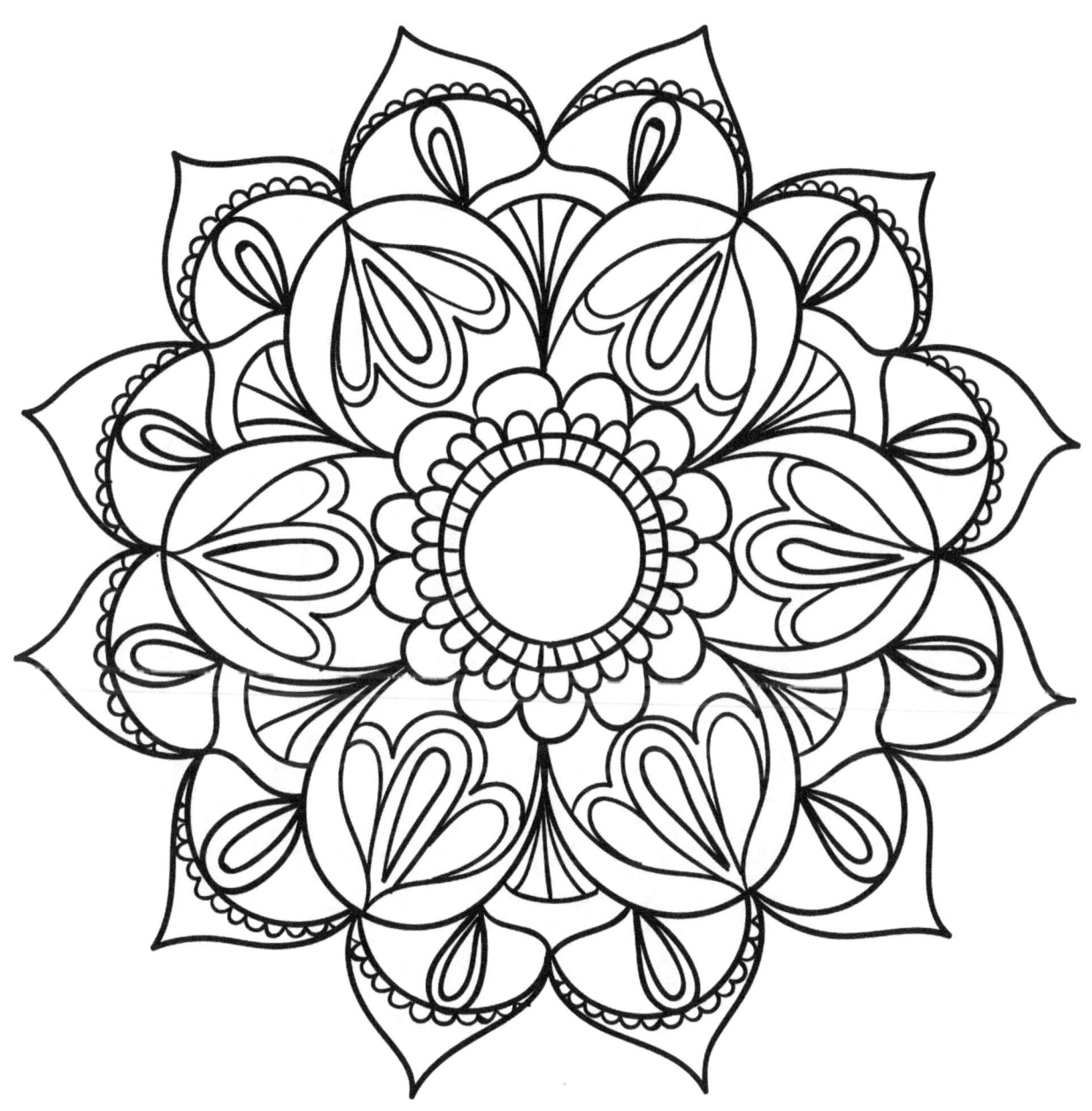

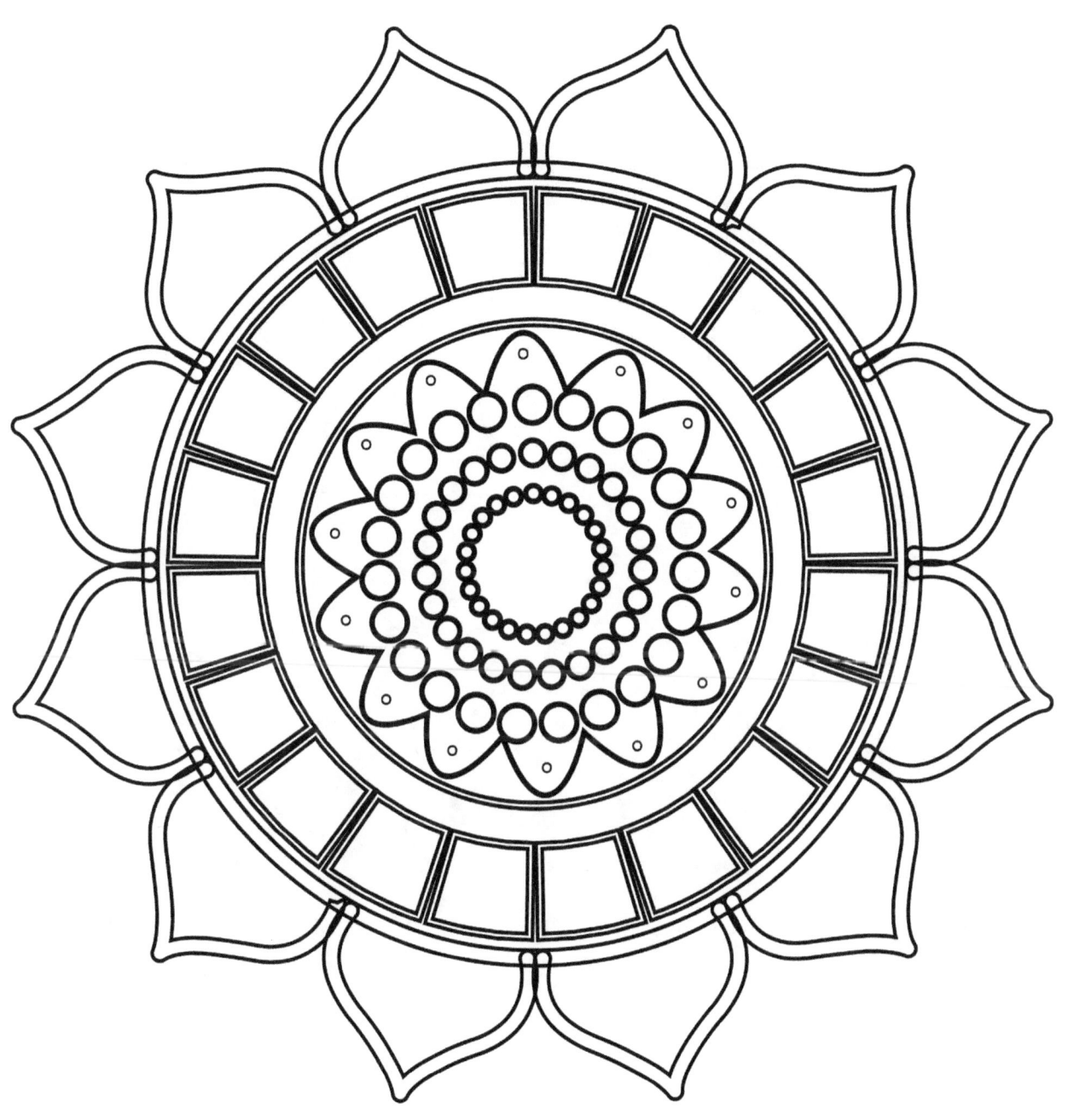

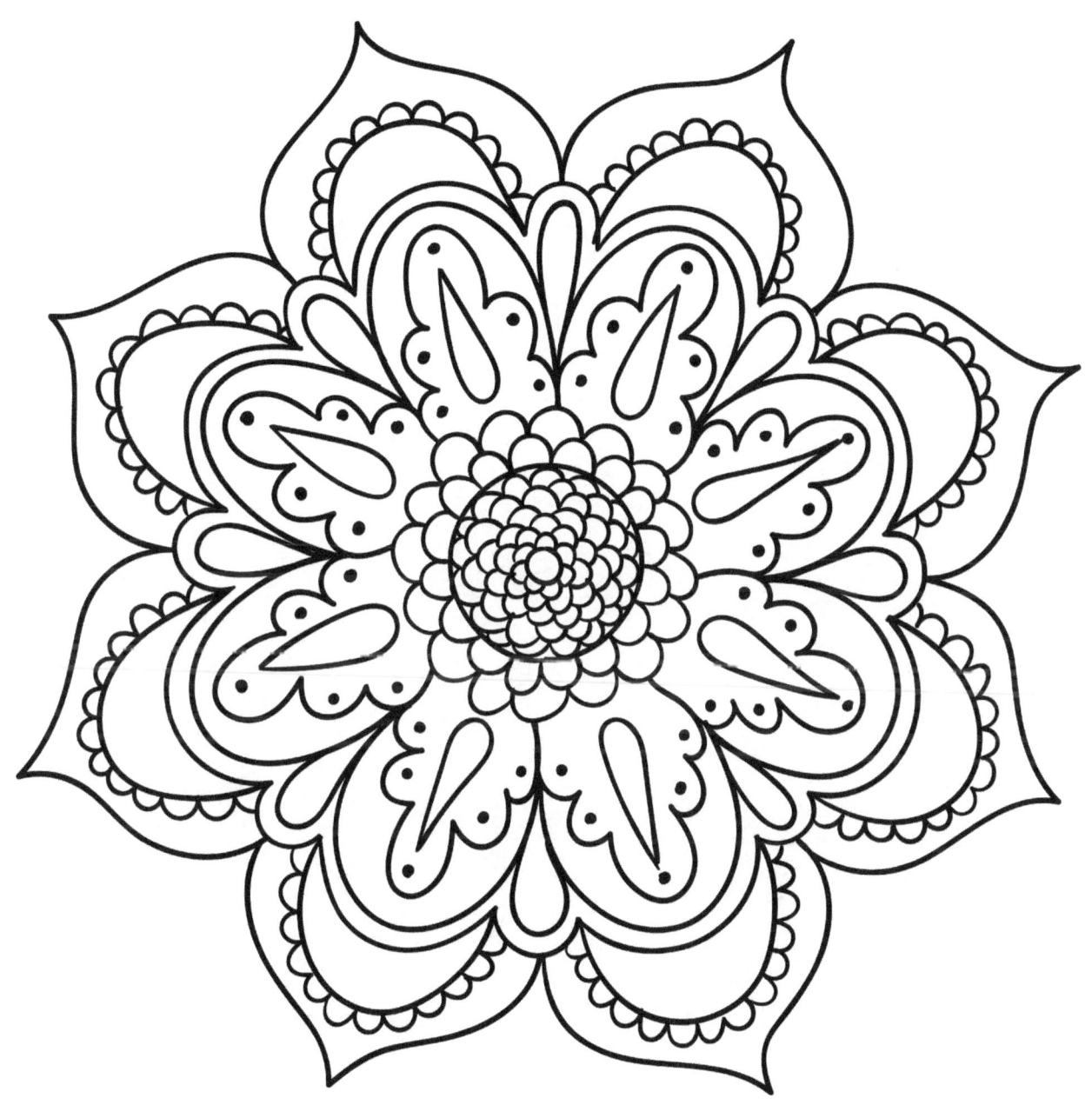

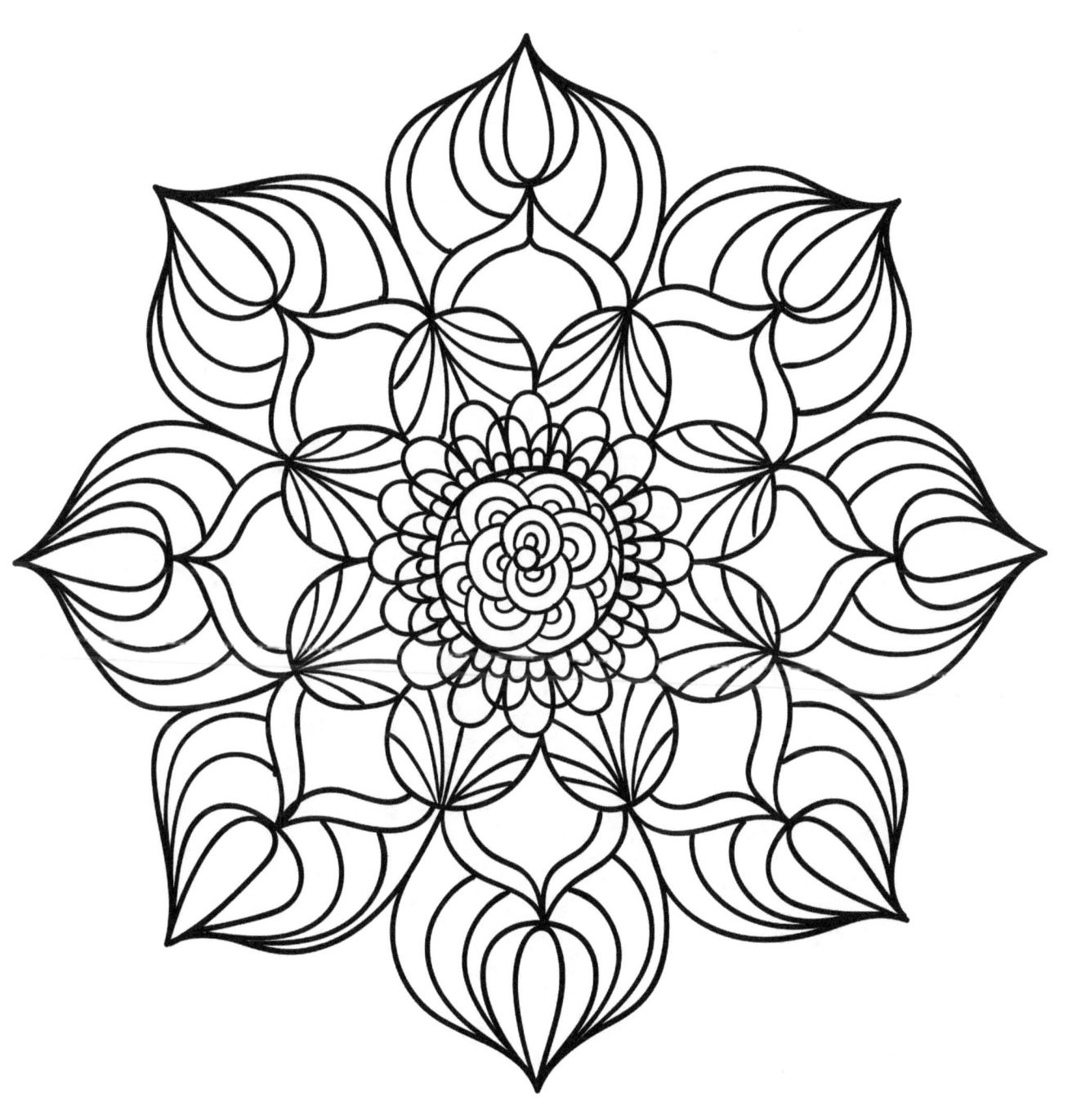

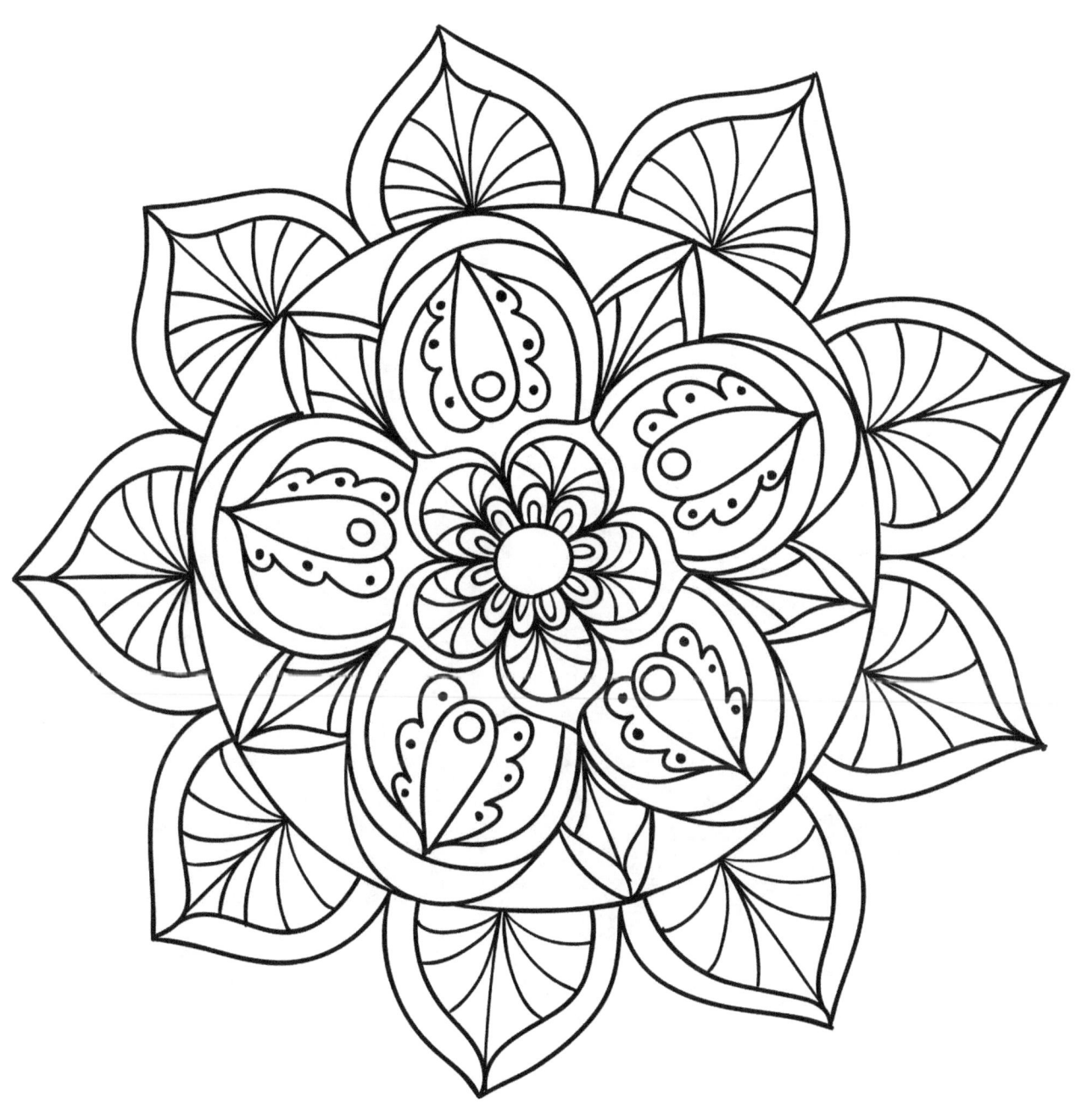

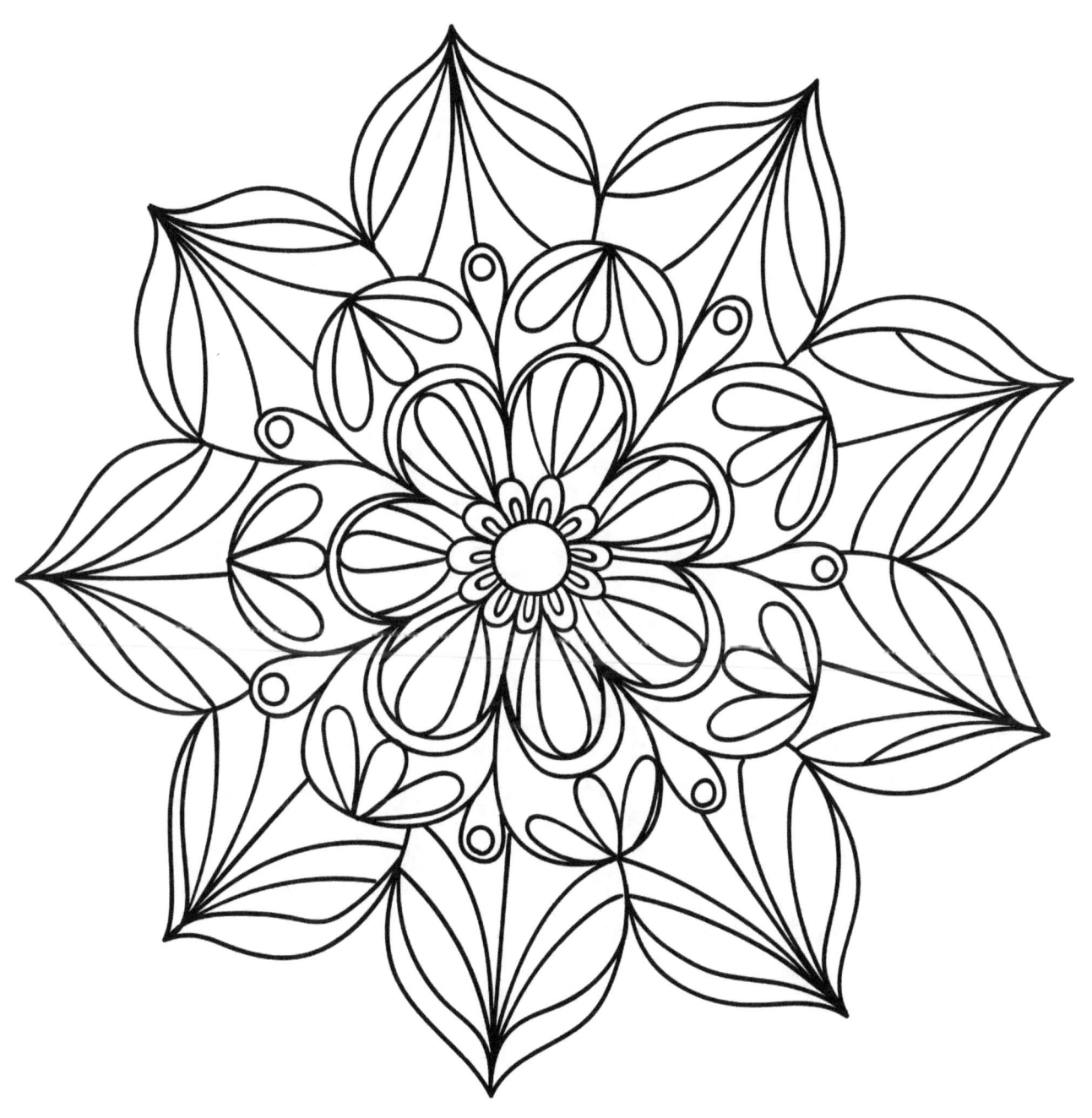

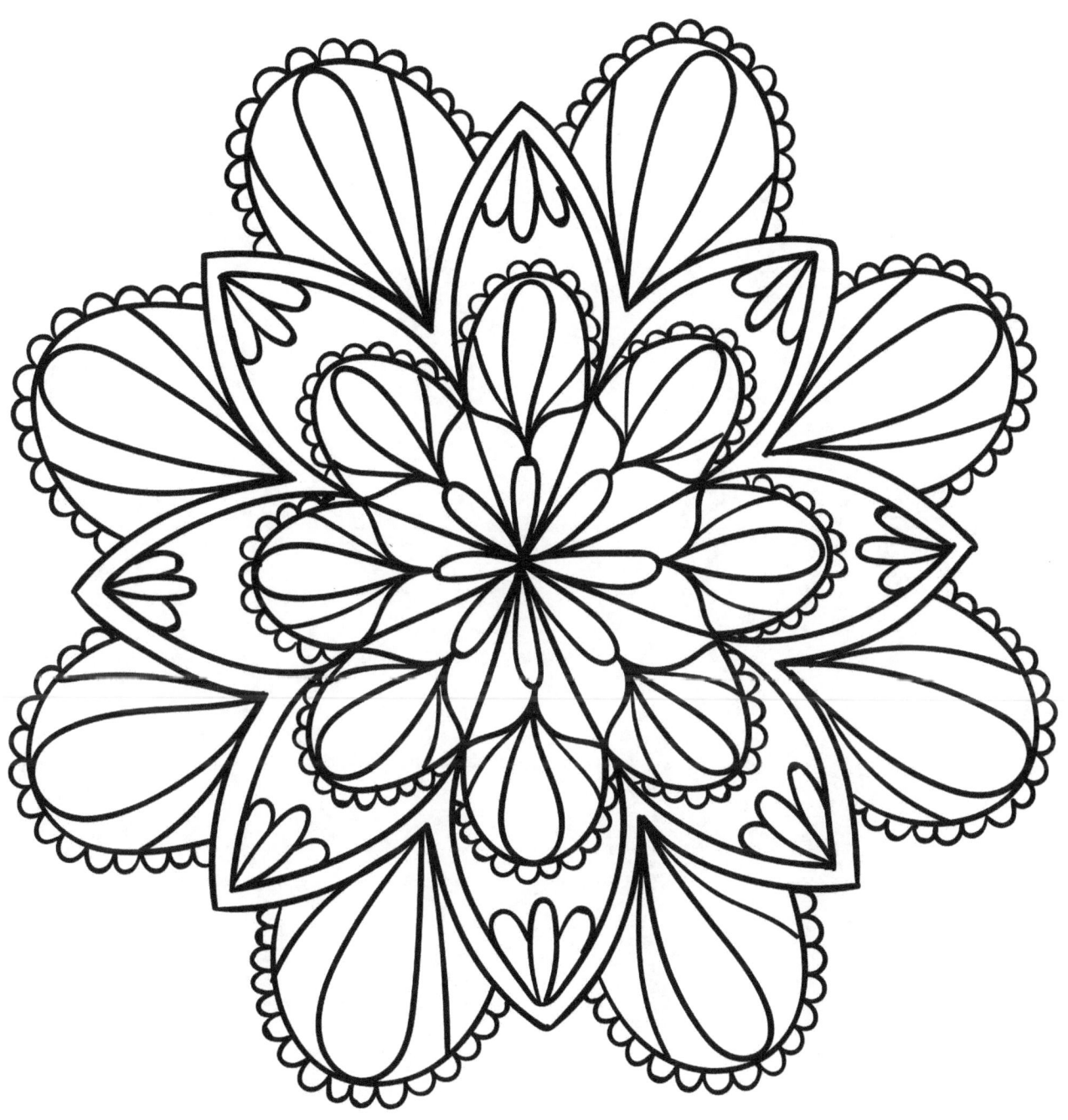

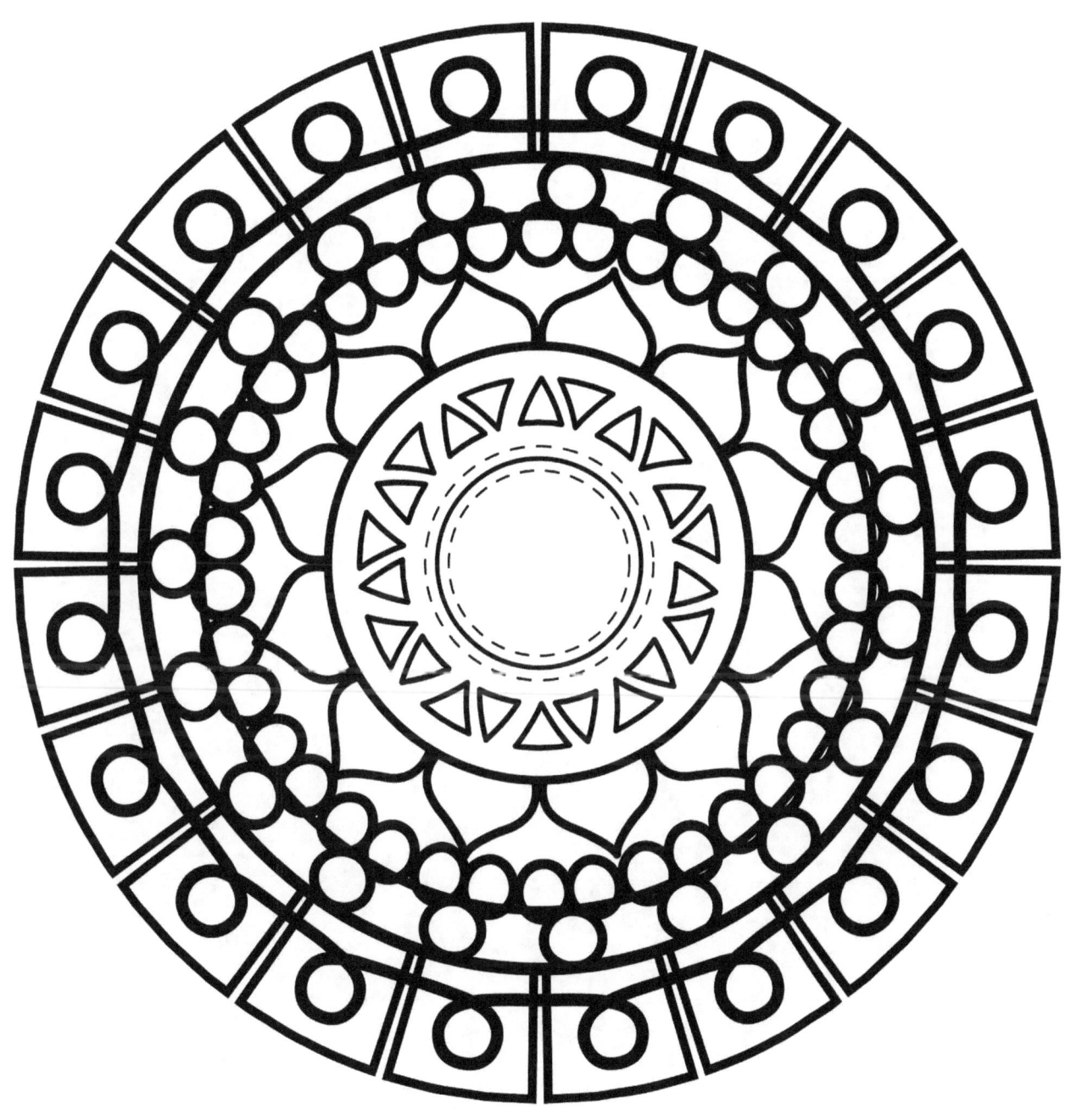

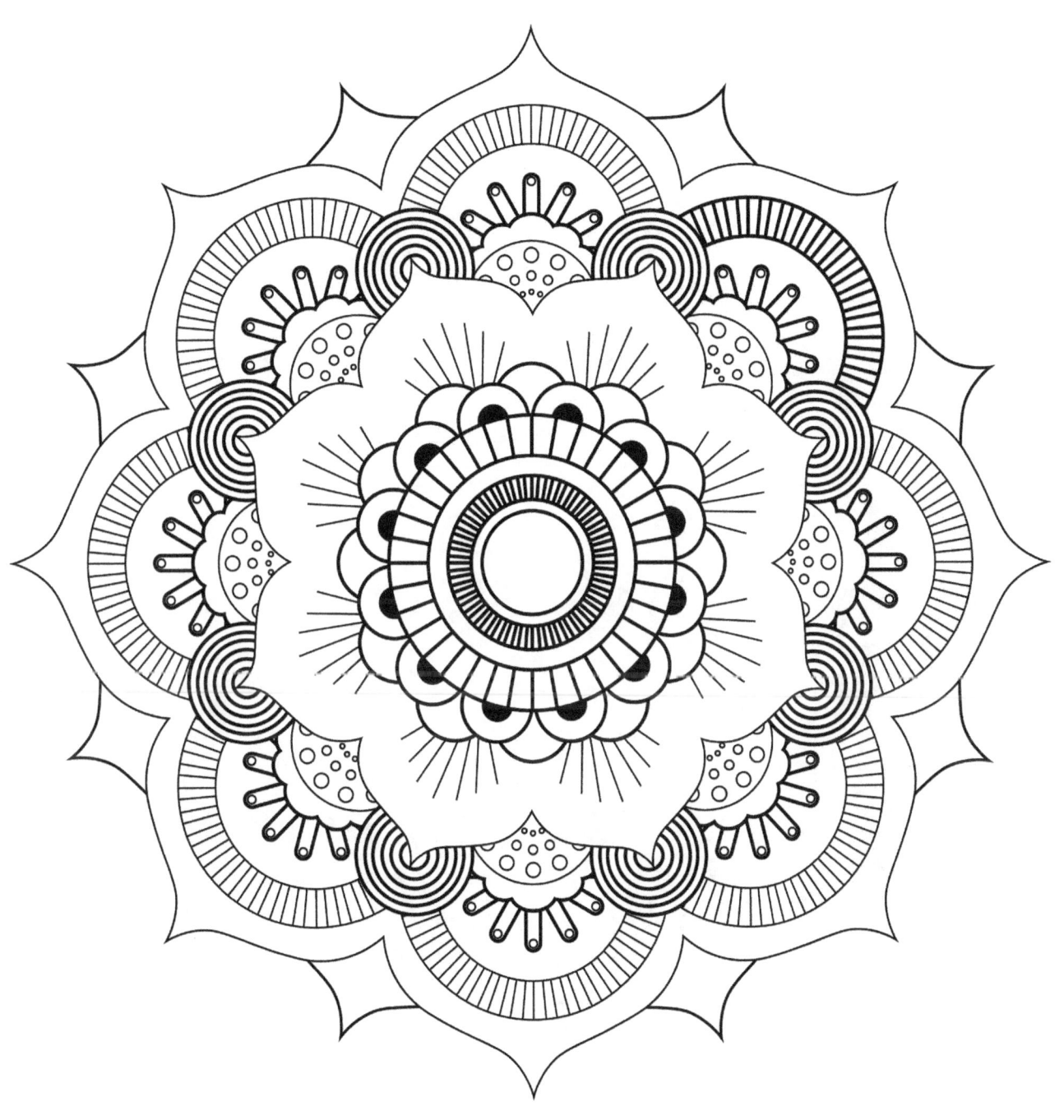

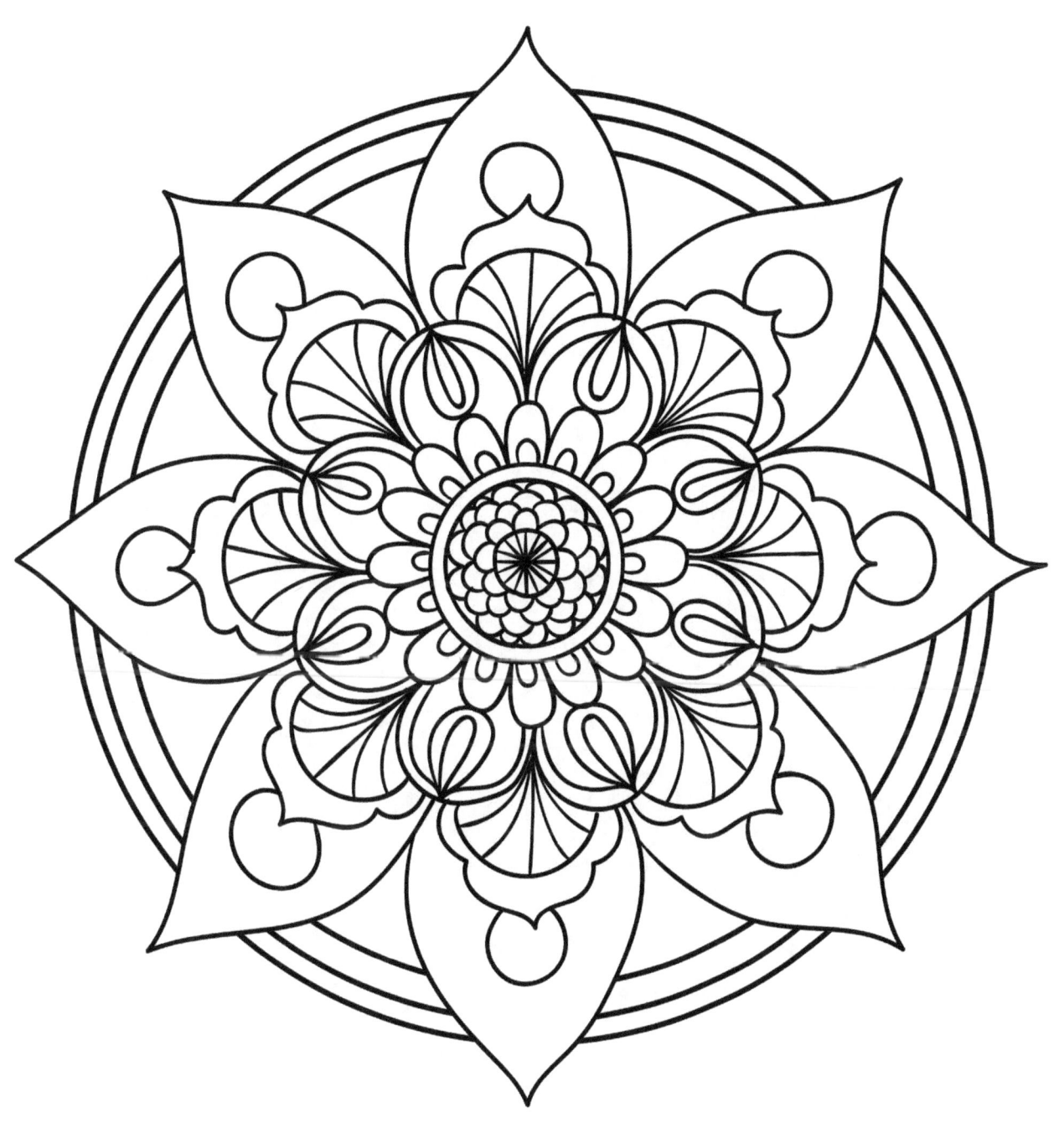

LOVED THIS BOOK?

Share us your colorful artwork!
http://www.KymieEdwins.com

/Kymie-Edwins   @KymieEdwins   @KymieEdwins